"Christopher Pramuk's latest [...] stunning introduction to the l[...] tradition. Priming our theolog[...] sensuous language of poetry an[...] [...]ons poem *Hagia Sophia* as a guide, Pramuk opens us to the divine music hidden in each of our encounters and allows us to glimpse the unseen Reality whom Merton calls Sophia. She is the breath of God poured out through the world, the one who shines from the faces of those who show courage and compassion in situations that cry for mercy. Pramuk explores her many manifestations within the Hebrew and Christian Scriptures and to people of various faith traditions, inviting us to peer into the liminal spaces of our own lives, the dark places, the places of our poverty where Sophia dwells and from which love springs. Myriad examples evidence the power of her presence and the depth of her love. This is a truly beautiful work, one that encourages deep contemplation of Sophia at work in our every encounter with Earth and with members of the human community and one that helps us to imagine how to speak of Christ in an age of pluralism."

— Kathleen Duffy, SSJ
    Author of *Teilhard's Mysticism: Seeing the Inner Face of Evolution*
    Professor of Physics and Director of the Institute
        for Religion and Science
    Chestnut Hill College, Philadelphia, Pennsylvania

"In the midst of this absolutely beautiful book of reflections on Wisdom in Thomas Merton, Christopher Pramuk asks, after citing a passage, 'Can somebody say Amen?!' Well, I can and am doing so with true delight. Pramuk brings together in his writing the poet and the scholar, the artist and the critic, the monk and prophet Merton was. His study of Wisdom in Merton is outstanding. This collection of reflections is a feast; Wisdom truly has set her table for us in them."

— Michael Plekon, PhD
    Professor, Sociology/Anthropology, Coordinator
        of the Program in Religion & Culture
    Baruch College of the City University of New York

"Born of Christopher Pramuk's prayerful pondering, and in sharing his questions and questing with others through retreats and talks, *At Play in Creation* is a lovely and inviting journey through the Sophia/Wisdom tradition. The writings of Thomas Merton, Etty Hillesum, poets, musicians, theologians/mystics of the Russian Sophia/Wisdom and Jewish traditions become the lens for exploring the Divine in the midst of a humanity bent on self-destruction. I found this oddly hope-filled and energizing. We *can* be the change we want to see in the world."

— Laura Swan, OSB
    Author of *The Benedictine Tradition* and *Wisdom of the Beguines: The Forgotten Story of a Medieval Women's Movement*

"In Christopher Pramuk's marvelous new book, lyrical theology and thoughtfully grounded spirituality merge into one. His 'voice' resonates in harmony with Thomas Merton's. As a professor of theology, Pramuk reads Merton well, but then as poet and musician, he sings and plays with Merton's most significant themes in a fresh, new key. He hovers widely over Merton's texts and darts after moments of beauty that represent Merton's lived affirmation of the Divine Feminine, *Hagia Sophia*, as deeply implicated in Merton's hopes for the world's ultimate salvation. Pramuk lures his reader to appreciate Holy Wisdom's epiphany among us as mercy and loving kindness, even as we experience the gaze of Sorrow's face; Sophia is the divine blessing who grounds our renewal in the Spirit, even in the face of everything that is failing us. Pramuk is now my go-to theologian/poet for a trustworthy rendition of Merton's legacy. I smell a 'classic' about to be born before my grateful eyes."

— Jonathan Montaldo
    Author of *Bridges to Contemplative Living with Thomas Merton*

At Play in Creation

Merton's Awakening
to the Feminine Divine

Christopher Pramuk

LITURGICAL PRESS
Collegeville, Minnesota

www.litpress.org

Cover design by Ann Blattner. Front cover image by Thomas Merton. Used with permission of the Merton Legacy Trust and the Thomas Merton Center, Bellarmine University. Back cover photo: © The Estate of Ralph Eugene Meatyard, courtesy Fraenkel Gallery, San Francisco.

| 2 | 3 | 4 | 5 | 6 | 7 | 8 | 9 |

Library of Congress Control Number: 2014947788

ISBN 978-0-8146-4816-2   978-0-8146-4841-4 (ebook)

To my mother Gladys Pramuk,
    poet, woman of strength, friend

And to my son Isaiah, gentle and wise,
    who shares his birthday with Thomas Merton

The experience of a great mystic is always paradoxical, even disquieting, to any system. . . . Over the centuries the "friends" of Job have polished and honed their concepts until they possess an amazing perfection of logical clarity. "In this system . . . widespread everywhere today, God is not killed; He is assimilated." . . . In such "organized reality," the Gospel paradox, with its explosive truth, is conjured away.

> ~ Paul Evdokimov,
> *The Feminine and the Salvation of the World*

All categories and classifications fold
when Presence fills the spaces of the soul.

Love loves, speaks Love,
all loves and all is well.

> ~ Susan McCaslin, "Night of Ecstasy"

Gentleness comes to him when he is most helpless and awakens him, refreshed, beginning to be made whole. Love takes him by the hand, and opens to him the door to another life, another day.

> ~ Thomas Merton, *Hagia Sophia*

Contents

O Wisdom, you came forth from the mouth
  of the Most High,
and reaching from the beginning to end,
you ordered all things mightily and sweetly.
Come, and teach us the way of prudence.

~ O Antiphon for Advent

Introduction

Merton and Sophia

*T*his small book represents the distillation of many years of reflection on Wisdom-Sophia, the feminine manifestation of God's presence in the world, who speaks and sings in the life and writings of Trappist monk and spiritual writer Thomas Merton. Since the publication of my book *Sophia: The Hidden Christ of Thomas Merton*, I have been invited to present its major ideas in various settings before diverse audiences. Most of these gatherings have taken place at retreat centers and churches, a few at academic conferences. The present book is the fruit of my preparation for these gatherings but also of the many grace-filled conversations I've shared with participants at them. Though the written word cannot capture the spontaneity and sheer gift to me of engaging this material with strangers and new friends alike, I hope the reader will discern in these pages something of the music, and the quickening of hope, which I have felt on these occasions. Wisdom is like that, it seems. She comes alive in the dance itself, in the pregnant spaces between speech and silence, solitude and community, delighting in God's creation and in the simplest acts of presence, vulnerability, and love between people.

My first aim in preparing these "retreat conferences" has been to offer a compact crystallization of the book's major themes but in a more narrative, poetic, and personal key than I was able to do in *Sophia*, which is set largely as an academic study.[1] A second aim, no less vital for me, was to extend the book's exploration of the deep question of God into realms of memory and experience that lay beyond Merton's writings and beyond even an overtly religious framework. In other words, if the "sophianic" or Wisdom-haunted remembrance of God that rises from the deep matrix of Merton's life is authentic and truly real—if it is *trustworthy*—then we ought to be able to discern hints of her Real Presence breaking through in lives other than Merton's, including our own. Thus the heartbeat of these conferences is not Merton as such but Sophia, the presence and mercy of God "pervading all things" to which Merton's witness points, even where through a glass darkly.

Merton wrote for a generation reeling from the Second World War, the global nuclear threat, the American war in Vietnam, and explosive race riots, an era he called a "season of fury." Like Gandhi, Heschel, and King, he saw our social ills as symptoms of a deeply entrenched spiritual malaise, not least our clinging to dangerous idols and idolatrous conceptions of God. Against the desecration of God, of nature, and of human persons everywhere, Merton would interject the gentle voice of Sophia, "at once my own being, my own nature, and the Gift of my Creator's Thought and Art within me." And a piercing lament: "We do not hear the soft voice, the gentle voice, the merciful and feminine. . . . We do not see the Child who is prisoner in all the people."[2]

Ours is a generation not so distant from Merton's: disillusioned with institutional religion; mesmerized by technology; distracted and surfeited by entertainment; haunted by the specter of terrorism and routine eruptions of gun violence; crippled by war; fragmented by gaping economic, racial, and gender inequalities; and threatened in ways we cannot yet imagine by the looming environmental crisis. Where is God to be experienced in all this? Who is God? *Is* God? Who will speak words of hope, of renewed theological imagination, for the next generation? Sophia emerges in Merton's writings as the Love and Mercy of God at play in creation who calls out from beneath the fog of ignorance and violence and unites all things "like the air receiving the sunlight." But are we listening? Here is Merton's lament. "Lights on. Clocks ticking. Thermostats working. Stoves cooking. Electric shavers filling radios with static. 'Wisdom,' cries the dawn deacon, but we do not attend."[3]

All of this suggests a third aim for this book, admittedly more tenuous and more like an author's humble prayer: that these pages might stir in others what awakens in me as I engage Merton's dance with Sophia—a renewed sense of God's nearness and friendship, and above all a fierce hope, rising not from any formal "theology" as such but divined from the hidden matrices of life itself, Life made from Love. For Wisdom "cries out to all who will hear, and she cries out particularly to the little, to the ignorant and the helpless." If we desire to know her, Merton reassures us, she will speak to us "on all sides in everything,"[4] and we will never be the same again.

For all the words and books written by Thomas Merton, for all the words and books still being written about him, I think the man himself would be pleased if we remembered only this, which has also been said of St. Benedict, his monastic forebear: "He was a God-oriented man leading like-minded people on the way of the Gospel."[5] To know God, Merton would discover, is to know God as Father, Son, and Spirit, and also as Holy Wisdom: Mother, Sister, Child, Brother, and Friend. This book celebrates, as it were, the *wholeness* of God, the *freedom* of God's love as reflected in creation and in the lives of all God's people, shining with particular intensity in the life of Thomas Merton. Merton was a friend of God, whose witness draws us likewise into the dance of God's love, mercy, and friendship.

1

Rivers of Night

The night, O My Lord, is a time of freedom. You have seen the morning and the night, and the night was better. In the night all things began, and in the night the end of all things has come before me. Baptized in the rivers of night, Gethsemani has recovered her innocence. Darkness brings a semblance of order before all things disappear. With the clock slung over my shoulder, in the silence of the Fourth of July, it is my time to be the night watchman, in the house that will one day perish.[1]

So begins one of the most-celebrated passages in Thomas Merton's vast body of work, "Fire Watch, July 4, 1952," the epilogue to *The Sign of Jonas*. I was fifteen when I read these words for the first time. Merton's dialogue with silence and mystery struck me with the force of a revelation. Like many others before and since, I was hooked, and Merton became a kind of spiritual companion through my young adulthood. Even today, when I sink into "Fire Watch," it is like walking into the church of my childhood: the words steady my pulse, deepen my breath, slow my mind, and open my imagination. With Merton I see again, from a perch high atop the monastery, a great canopy of stars and feel the night wind on my face. I become small before the majesty and mystery of God. I pray like a child.

In this centenary year of Merton's birth, the words of "Fire Watch" seem to me a fitting entry point as we join with people around the world to remember and celebrate Merton's witness to faith and hopefulness in a troubled world. Like the monks of Gethsemani laying themselves down to sleep in the monastery, like Jonah, hiding from God in the belly of the whale, we too are "baptized in rivers of night," exiles "sailing to slavery, [yet still] hoping for glory."[2] We too are haunted by life "singing in the watercourses," stirred by ancient stories of a God who journeys with us through desert and darkness and promises to renew all creation with resurrection hope. Of course, the rhythms of Merton's life were suffused with all of these: word and silence, storytelling and song, labor and stillness, memory and hope. Like the biblical poets and prophets of old, Merton interrupts our habitual or half-tied vision of things, calling us back to ourselves, to our deepest identity in God, in one another, and in the natural world, before it is too late. As both a monk and an extraordinarily gifted writer, Merton helps us to hear again the music of our faith.

Most readers well acquainted with Merton will have a story to share, a favorite book or passage that got them "hooked" or still haunts their imagination. An elder African American woman and former nun in my parish once shared with me that *Conjectures of a Guilty Bystander* was her "Bible" during the 1960s, when she was an activist for racial justice and felt increasingly alienated by her religious community. "Merton *got it*," she said to me, with a somewhat pained look on her face, "when few others did." For many older readers it is Merton's autobiography, *The Seven Storey Mountain*, which marks a pivotal signpost or even a major turning point in their life's journey. For me, it was reading "Fire Watch" as a teenager, and then throughout my twenties his journals, *New Seeds of Contemplation*, and the incomparable *Raids on the Unspeakable*.

It is curious, however, that by my mid-thirties Merton's writings had drifted and all but disappeared from my consciousness. It wasn't until I began doctoral studies in theology—two years after September 11, 2001, and in the charged atmosphere surrounding the launch of the second Iraq war—that Merton reemerged with some force for me as a locus of real interest for the most pressing issues in theology and Christian spirituality today. Like many of my peers, I was fixed on the problem of how to speak of Christ in an age of religious pluralism and, to be sure, an era of increasing violence between cultures and nations. Merton had dedicated many years of study and witness to interfaith friendship and dialogue. Who is the Christ, I wondered, that centered Merton's outreach during the extraordinary last decade of his life? In whom did he find his deepest identity and place his prayerful trust? Who is the God of his intimate companionship and faith?

The more I studied, meditated on, and pored over his writings, the more I discerned an unmistakable music, a kind of unifying harmonic "key," awakening in me the remembrance of God, a sense of a real Presence, and stirring dormant seeds of hope. Above all it was Merton's prose poem *Hagia Sophia*, which, like a kind of magnetic north, drew my imagination back into itself, again and again. The flowering in Merton of years of study and meditation on the Bible, patristic and Russian Orthodox theology, and Zen, the poem seemed at once to multiply and silence all my questions. Rather than succumbing to my preconceived theological categories and preconceptions of God, it broke them open. To this day, there is a music in the poem that eludes all understanding for me, yet reverberates deeply when I surrender myself to its imagery.

Set according to the liturgical hours, the poem begins in a hospital room at dawn, where the speaker is awakened "out of languor and darkness" by the soft voice of a nurse. The experience is all gift, belying its setting in a place of disease and subjugation to machines, for in "the cool hand of the nurse there is the touch of all life, the touch of Spirit."

Dawn. The Hour of Lauds

There is in all visible things an invisible fecundity, a dimmed light, a meek namelessness, a hidden wholeness. This mysterious Unity and Integrity is Wisdom, the Mother of all, *Natura naturans*. There is in all things an inexhaustible sweetness and purity, a silence that is a fount of action and joy. It rises up in wordless gentleness and flows out to me from the unseen roots of all created being, welcoming me tenderly, saluting me with indescribable humility. This is at once my own being, my own nature, and the Gift of my Creator's Thought and Art within me, speaking as Hagia Sophia, speaking as my sister, Wisdom.[3]

The poem has haunted me for years, and I have struggled and broken my head trying to get inside the text to explain its particular magic. But there is nothing to explain, and no magic; there is only the music of divine Mercy, realized in each of us according to our willingness to receive it.

O blessed, silent one, who speaks everywhere!

We do not hear the soft voice, the gentle voice, the merciful and feminine.

We do not hear mercy, or yielding love, or non-resistance, or non-reprisal. In her there are no reasons and no answers. Yet she is the candor of God's light, the expression of His simplicity.[4]

If it is true, as the late Fr. Andrew Greeley writes, that "the artist is a sacrament maker, a creator of emphasized, clarified beauty designed to make us see,"[5] then Merton in *Hagia Sophia* is the consummate artist, helping us to see—that is, to *feel* in our whole person—that while the world is stricken deeply by sin, it is also limned in the light of resurrection.

Sophia is the *eros* of God become one with all creation, the love in God that longs for incarnation from before the beginning. She is the co-creativity of God, always inviting, never compelling, coming to birth in us when we say yes to "the dawning of divine light in the stillness of our hearts."[6] She is the invitation to the wedding dance, and at once the Bride and the Feast and the Wedding. In a century of unspeakable violence and fragmentation, *Hagia Sophia* is Merton's most lyric expression of "Christ being born into the whole world,"[7] especially in that which is most "poor" and "hidden." It is his consummate hymn to peace.

That the poem came to birth in an era Merton described as a "season of fury" is not incidental. Half a century earlier, in the Russian Orthodox East, she had haunted the imaginations of mystics, artists, and intellectuals caught in the throes of the Bolshevik Revolution and two devastating world wars, a time of total war and massive human displacement. As for the Russian theologians of Sophia, so it was for Thomas Merton. Indeed, it is impossible to separate Merton's awakening to Sophia or any aspect of his spiritual autobiography from the remarkable century in which he lived. Let us briefly review the broad tapestry of Merton's life, which will prepare us in the next conference to reflect on a number of classic texts from his extraordinary body of work.[8]

Merton was born in France in 1915 to Ruth Jenkins, from America, and Owen Merton, from New Zealand, itinerant artists who had met in Paris. By the time Merton was sixteen, both of his parents were dead. His account of the loss of his mother when he was six years old is one of the most poignant passages in *The Seven Storey Mountain*, clearly affecting him profoundly.[9] Perhaps, as not a few have wondered, it set Merton forth unconsciously "on a lifelong quest for the feminine."[10] But there was also, many years later, the loss of his younger brother,

John Paul, killed in a bomber crash during the Second World War, remembered in a stirring poem that concludes the autobiography: "Sweet brother, if I do not sleep / My eyes are flowers for your tomb."[11] The "flowers of paradise" were indelibly scented for Merton, from a very early age, with the loneliness of loss and suffering.

Merton's godfather, Dr. Tom Bennett, became his guardian when Merton was sixteen, in the wake of his father's death. Merton completed his studies at Oakham School in England and then enrolled at Cambridge. His raucous behavior there led to his being sent back to the United States, where he enrolled at Columbia in New York City and soon thrived among an *avant-garde* and literary group of friends: Robert Lax, Ed Rice, Sy Freedgood, and his teacher and mentor Mark van Doren. At Columbia Merton's reading became "more and more Catholic." Reading Etienne Gilson's *The Spirit of Medieval Philosophy* was transformative. He devoured works by Blake, Hopkins, Joyce, and Maritain. As Merton later described this period, something deep "began to stir within me . . . began to push me, to prompt me . . . like a voice."[12] To the shock of many of his friends, he announced his desire to become a Roman Catholic and was baptized on November 16, 1938, at Corpus Christi Church in New York City. In September 1940, Merton began teaching English at St. Bonaventure in New York. After spending Holy Week of 1941 on retreat at the Abbey of Gethsemani in the hills of rural Western Kentucky, Merton decided to become a Trappist monk.

How to account for this extraordinary turn of events? In fact, the seeds for Merton's conversion had been planted some years earlier, when Merton was eighteen and visiting Rome, as described in a memorable passage in *The Seven Storey Mountain*. An orphan in the world, he found himself drawn into the city's ancient churches. In one of these he was overwhelmed by "a great mosaic, in the apse, of Christ's coming in judgment in a dark blue sky, with the suggestions of fire in the small clouds beneath his feet."[13] Something stirred within the teenaged Merton as he wandered into these sacred spaces and gazed on the Byzantine mosaics that adorned their walls.

> And now for the first time in my life I began to find out something of Who this Person was that men called Christ. It was obscure, but it was a true knowledge of Him, in some sense, truer than I knew and truer than I would admit. But it was in Rome that my conception of Christ was formed. It was there that I first saw Him, Whom I now serve as my God and my King and Who owns and rules my life.[14]

It is significant that Merton describes his knowledge of Christ in these early encounters as "a true knowledge," even if it "was obscure." The dormant seeds of his faith had been stirred, significantly, through an immersion in a cultural landscape quite different from his own. But there is more. It is fair to intuit that in gazing on these ancient mosaics and icons Merton had felt himself *the object of Christ's gaze* for the first time in his life. It seems there was something in the eyes of Christ resonating in the eyes of Merton's heart, coming toward him, as it were, speaking to him. A few nights later, a similar kind of presence came to him.

I was in my room. It was night. The light was on. Suddenly it seemed to me that [my] Father, who had been dead more than a year, was there with me. The sense of his presence was as vivid and as real and as startling as if he had touched my arm or spoken to me. The whole thing passed in a flash, but in that flash . . . I was overwhelmed with a sudden and profound insight into the misery and corruption of my own soul, and I was pierced deeply with a light that made me realize something of the condition I was in. . . .

And now I think for the first time I really began to pray—praying . . . out of the very roots of my life and of my being, and praying to the God I had never known, to reach down towards me out of His darkness and to help me get free of the thousand terrible things that held my will in their slavery.[15]

The following day Merton returned to the Church of Santa Sabina to pray. Self-conscious and afraid he might be thrown out, he nevertheless prayed, feeling as though he had been reborn. It would be several years before he found himself drawn back into a church, this time to Corpus Christi, near Columbia, and five years before he would become a Catholic on November 16, 1938.

From 1941 to 1968 Merton lived as a monk of Gethsemani. It was the publication of *The Seven Storey Mountain* in 1948 that established him as a famous monk and a wholly unexpected literary phenomenon. In addition to publishing widely read spiritual meditations, journals, and poetry, during the last decade of his life Merton would write penetrating essays on the most explosive social issues of the day, the religions of the East, monastic and church reform, and questions of belief and atheism. Above all, he made the case for the contemplative life in a world of relentless action.

Several other experiences profoundly shaped Merton's life as a monk and spiritual writer. Between 1955 and 1965 he served as master of novices, helping the young monks imbibe from the deepest wellsprings of the Christian mystical tradition. Always meticulously prepared, he clearly loved his students and taught them with great spontaneity, energy, and humor. In 1965 Merton received permission to live as a hermit on the grounds of the monastery, which freed his spirit and voice in new ways. Much of his best writing comes to us from the hermitage. During a hospital stay in Louisville in the spring of 1966, Merton fell in love with a young student nurse named Margie, or "M.," as she is rendered in the journals. For some six months they had a kind of clandestine affair until, with considerable anguish and regret, Merton finally broke it off, helped not a little by his abbot's discovery of the affair. The relationship was transformative for Merton and bears a spiritual significance that we will revisit later.

In October 1968 Merton set out for Asia on what would be his final pilgrimage, desiring "to drink from [the] ancient sources of monastic vision and experience."[16] He dreamed of meeting the Dalai Lama and fulfilling what he believed to be the vocation of every Christian: to be an instrument of unity, to "realize the unity that already is and to find ways to live together that are consistent with unity."[17] It would be difficult to name another twentieth-century Christian who sought after this vision more tenaciously, publically, and prophetically than Thomas Merton. The fruits of his outreach are still being realized today in many who have found courage and grace in his example.

Merton died in Bangkok on December 10, 1968, the victim of an accidental electrocution and probably a resultant heart attack. His body was returned to the United States in a military transport plane that was carrying the bodies of servicemen killed in Vietnam, a war he had condemned forcefully. His body was laid in the earth on a hillside behind the monastery, overlooking the Kentucky woods where he lived as a hermit the last years of his life. Pilgrims continue to visit and pray before the simple white cross that marks Merton's grave.

11

Liminal Spaces

Merton has rightly been described as a prophet and peacemaker. But readers continue to marvel at the breadth and beauty with which Merton's peacemaking extends beyond the human community to embrace the natural world. Merton's "sapiential," "sophianic," or Wisdom-haunted way of seeing—imbued with an intuitive and holistic sense of communion with God in all things—seems to come most alive and virtually leap off the page when he is immersed in nature. Consider Merton's "Prayer to God the Father on the Vigil of Pentecost," from *Conjectures of a Guilty Bystander*:

> Today, Father, this blue sky lauds you. The delicate green and orange flowers of the tulip poplar tree praise you. The distant blue hills praise you, together with the sweet-smelling air that is full of brilliant light. The bickering flycatchers praise you with the lowing cattle and the quails that whistle over there. I too, Father, praise you, with all these my brothers, and they give voice to my own heart and to my own silence. We are all one silence, and a diversity of voices. . . .

Here I am. In me the world is present, and you are present.
I am a link in the chain of light and of presence.[1]

Note the repetition of the phrase "I am"—words with deep
biblical resonance, as in God's self-revelation to Moses at the
burning bush (Exod 3:14). Note as well Merton's seeming disappearance into a communion beyond subject and object, beyond
the split between observer and one being observed. What Merton describes in his writings on nature and invites us to share
is not a series of isolated "peak experiences," here one moment,
gone the next. Rather, Merton initiates us into an encounter with
reality, a whole-bodied *communion* with nature, a "realization"
that is in time but also beyond time, touching the eternal. *We are
all one silence, and a diversity of voices.*[2] Consider another passage,
one of my favorites in all his journals, this from August 25, 1958:

> The grip the *present* has on me. That is the one thing that
> has grown most noticeably in the spiritual life. . . . The
> rest dims as it should. I am getting older. The reality of
> *now*—the unreality of all the rest. The unreality of ideas
> and explanations and formulas. I am. The unreality of
> all the rest. The pigs shriek. Butterflies dance together
> . . . against the blue sky at the end of the woodshed. The
> buzzsaw stands outside there, half covered with dirty and
> tattered canvas. The trees are fresh and green in the sun
> (more rain yesterday). Small clouds inexpressibly beautiful
> and silent and eloquent, over the silent woodlands. What a
> celebration of light, quietness, and glory! This is my feast,
> sitting here in the straw!

At Mass, sad inmates of Dachau, Auschwitz, Vorkuta, Solovki, Novolsk, Karajanda, stood triumphantly by the altar at the commemoration of the dead.[3]

Notice the pregnant paradoxes: Merton is alone yet not alone. Surrounded by grasses and trees, birds and spring flowers, embraced in silence and solitude, Merton bodily *feels* the surrounding environment. But there is more. He feels too, and palpably, the presence of the dead, the cloud of witnesses, those who have gone before. "At Mass, sad inmates of Dachau, Auschwitz, Vorkuta . . . stood triumphantly by the altar at the commemoration of the dead."

Merton is a poet of the liminal spaces of our lives, those moments we find ourselves "in between," passing through a kind of doorway to touch the eternal. The word "liminal" derives from the Latin "limen," meaning "threshold." Merton's writings are suffused with what Christian theology calls the realm of "eschatology"—from *eschaton*, or the "last things"—that fertile paradox in Christian life between our pilgrimage in history now, on this side of death, and our hope for an all-embracing fulfillment yet to come. Among Merton's most celebrated passages it would be hard to find a single one that did not reflect the tensive insertion of our lives in the boundary between present and future, "moving back and forth between them, tasting here and now 'in this body, . . . in this vessel' some piece of heaven, a foretaste, a 'pledge.'"[4] Consider one of the best-known in Merton's corpus, his unexpected "epiphany" at the crossroads of Fourth and Walnut in Louisville, on March 18, 1958:

In Louisville, at the corner of Fourth and Walnut, in the center of the shopping district, I was suddenly overwhelmed with the realization that I loved all those people, that they were mine and I theirs, that we could not be alien to one another even though we were total strangers. It was like waking from a dream of separateness, of spurious self-isolation in a special world, the world of renunciation and supposed holiness. . . .

This sense of liberation from an illusory difference was such a relief and such a joy to me that I almost laughed out loud. . . . Thank God, thank God that I *am* like other [human beings], that I am only a [human being] among others. . . . It is a glorious destiny to be a member of the human race, though it is a race dedicated to many absurdities and one which makes many terrible mistakes: yet, with all that, God Himself gloried in becoming a member of the human race. A member of the human race! . . . As if the sorrows and stupidities of the human condition could overwhelm me, now I realize what we all are. And if only everybody could realize this! But it cannot be explained. There is no way of telling people that they are all walking around shining like the sun.[5]

Up to now Merton had viewed his vocation in the traditional way as a "flight from the world" (*fuga mundi*), setting him apart in a kind of separate, holy existence from the masses of humanity. This conception of holiness, which privileged the clerical life and reflected a sharp dualism in modern Catholic thought between the sacred and the secular, was about to change radically for Merton, as it was for the whole church at Vatican II. Here Merton was discovering the lightning flash of God in *the stranger*, the worldly "other" who was once alien and even threatening to his monastic vocation. While this intuition of radical communion with the other is always "there" in the roots of our being, the gift has at the same time "been lost and must be recovered," suggests Merton. The recovery of our original "innocence"[6] requires a way back home, a spiritual discipline that interrupts our habitual ways of thinking and cultivates an awareness of *who we already are in God and in one another*, our kinship with all things in the "hidden ground of Love."[7]

The key to this epiphany of human life as the life story of God, says Merton, is *love*, the highest expression of spirituality and freedom. Love "is the work not of states, not of organizations, not of institutions, but of persons."[8] The love of God springs forth again and again, like a mustard seed, from the most hidden and unpromising places, indeed, sometimes from the darkest and most painful of human realities. As the Canadian singer Leonard Cohen puts it, it is very often through the cracks in the vessel, the terribly broken places in our lives, that the light can break in.[9]

To say it another way, the incarnation is not for Merton something that simply happened in the past, pointing to a beautiful and even morally compelling narrative about a God "out there" who comes down from heaven for a while and then goes back up to watch over and judge us. Merton helps us to grasp the incarnation as an ongoing event, something real, more than literally real, in the choices that make up our everyday lives. Every Christian, Merton reminds us, is a pilgrim on the road to

Emmaus: "We follow Him, we find Him . . . and then He must vanish and we must go along without Him at our side. Why? Because He is even closer than that. He is *ourself*."[10]

One of Merton's central concerns is that people in modern society have lost touch with the depth dimension of reality (what Jewish philosopher Martin Buber famously called the "I/Thou" mode of *encounter*) in favor of an analytical mode that engages the world by collecting data through our senses; analyzing, naming, and categorizing that data; and then developing theories about it (what Buber calls the "I/It" mode of *experience*).[11] We have traded mystery and wonder for mastery and technological manipulation, for cheap imitations of the real thing. The result is the deep sense of alienation so many feel amid mass society. To be alienated is to feel oneself *cut off* from all the "others," who feel equally isolated in the churning wheel of experience; cut off from the natural world, increasingly subjugated to utilitarian ends; and cut off from "God," who becomes a projection of our own sense of aloneness in an infinitely receding universe.

While driving recently I heard a story on National Public Radio about the newest products being showcased at an annual technology show in Las Vegas. One of the big software companies was trumpeting a kind of "virtual helmet" worn over the head that can "transport" the user into any environment of their choosing. The tech reporter spoke with great excitement about a program that would take the wearer of the virtual helmet into (ready for it?) Thoreau's *Walden Pond*, enabling the user to "see and hear everything Thoreau saw, the different birds and species of trees, the water lapping over rocks at the bank of the pond, the frogs croaking, the wisp of the wind through the cabin windows," and so on. Now we can go "to the woods" and "suck out all the marrow of life," the reporter gleefully concluded, "without ever leaving our living room." I nearly crashed the car.

In a little book called *The Way of Chuang Tzu*, Merton chronicles the poignant words of Lao Tzu, a wandering sage of the sixth century BCE, to his distraught disciple. Lao Tzu says:

> A moment ago
> I looked into your eyes.
> I saw you were hemmed in
> By contradictions. Your words
> Confirm this.
> You are scared to death,
> Like a child who has lost
> Father and mother.
> You are trying to sound
> The middle of the ocean
> With a six-foot pole.
> You have got lost, and are trying
> To find your way back
> To your own true self.
> You find nothing
> But illegible signposts
> Pointing in all directions.
> I pity you.[12]

This is the tragedy that most concerns Merton in the last decade of his life: we run after "illegible signposts pointing in all directions," when that which we seek *already rests deep within us*, much nearer and deeper than we could ever fathom "with a six-foot pole."

As both a monk and a writer, Merton came to see it as part of his vocation to help his contemporaries learn how to "sound the ocean," that is, to reestablish contact with the hidden ground of Love at the center of our being. Contemplation is simply this: the practice of becoming aware of ourselves as living in communion with God, with the natural world, and with one another. Contemplation is the art of being awake, of being deeply attuned to reality, here, now, in the present moment. It is, as Jesuit Walter Burghardt writes, "a long loving look at the real,"[13] where reality is neither abstract nor manufactured, not the kind of "real" one typically experiences through the lens of a television screen or an elaborate computer program. Contemplation is God's own gift of self, freely given. And yet this free gift implies on our part a painful letting go, a "putting to death" of our old, false self, necessary to make way for the "true self" God calls each of us to be.[14]

Here we might call to mind two contemporaries for whom Merton held the greatest admiration: Mahatma Gandhi and Martin Luther King Jr. What Merton describes as the "Indian mind that was awakening in Gandhi"[15] was not far from King's seminal belief in the "interrelated structure of all reality," a conviction rooted in King's biblical faith that a divine, loving presence binds all life together in "an inescapable network of mutuality," a "single garment of destiny."[16] In his darkest moments of doubt, fear, and despair, King felt this Presence reassuring and beckoning him forward, giving him courage and strength to love.

During an informal talk in Calcutta in October 1968, just over a month before his death, Merton described the character of this "I/Thou" communion across seemingly impassible boundaries: "It is wordless. It is beyond words, and it is beyond speech, and it is beyond concept. Not that we discover a new unity. We discover an older unity. My dear brothers, we are already one. But we imagine that we are not. And what we have to recover is our original unity. What we have to be is what we are."[17] Fully a decade earlier, Merton had struggled to express the same paradoxical experience of unity he shared with Zen scholar D. T. Suzuki: "The fact that you are a Zen Buddhist and I am a Christian monk, far from separating us, makes us most like one another. How many centuries is it going to take for people to discover this fact?"[18]

Here again Merton accompanies us into the boundaries that divide us from the "Other," the unfamiliar objects of our fears. Having prayed and studied with Merton for so long it seems to me that sustained exposure to his writings is not unlike being formed in the mystagogical climate of the liturgy itself. Merton trains our minds and hearts to open, attuning our spiritual senses to the transcendent dimension of reality, the divine music hidden in potentially every human experience, even, perhaps especially, those that carry us outside our comfort zone. To the degree we surrender ourselves to the text (or whole situation) at hand, the self-preoccupied "false self" recedes and something like music begins to break through.[19] Awakening in mystery to our essential kinship with the whole cosmos—or better, every rock, every creature and person, every blade of grass within it— ordinary things are made truly extraordinary in the light of God's grace. To be "bitten by Merton" is to be initiated into a world of revelation, heightened expectation, and presence.

A spirituality shaped by a robust sacramental imagination sees that while the world is stricken deeply by sin, it is also limned in the light of resurrection. And in this "general dance"[20] between God and the world, the human person mysteriously holds a special place as image and icon of God. Here the Wisdom literature of the Bible boldly, almost recklessly, celebrates the connecting threads—the liminal spaces!—between God, the cosmos, and the human race "from before the very beginning." And here Merton and the Russian Orthodox theologians of Wisdom from whom Merton would imbibe so deeply—as we shall see in the next conference—took their cues especially from Proverbs 8, where Sophia, the feminine Wisdom Child, emerges as a kind of "go-between" in creation.[21]

> The LORD begot me, the beginning of his works,
>   the forerunner of his deeds of long ago;
> From of old I was formed,
>   at the first, before the earth.
> When there were no deeps I was brought forth,
>   when there were no fountains or springs of water;
> Before the mountains were settled into place,
>   before the hills, I was brought forth;
> When the earth and the fields were not yet made,
>   nor the first clods of the world.
> When he established the heavens, there was I,
>   when he marked out the vault over the face of the deep;

When he made firm the skies above,
    when he fixed fast the springs of the deep;
When he set for the sea its limit,
    so that the waters should not transgress his command;
When he fixed the foundations of earth,
    then was I beside him as artisan;
I was his delight day by day,
    playing before him all the while,
Playing over the whole of his earth,
    having my delight with human beings.
                              (Prov 8:22-31; NABRE)

I was brought forth, I was there, I was beside him—from Bulgakov in the East to Merton in the West the Christian Wisdom tradition hears in these lines the music of an expansive divine-human mystery, a dual hymn evoking not only the presence of Christ, the uncreated Wisdom of God who orders and "plays" in the universe, but also, through Christ's humanity, as it were, the primordial presence of the human race, created Sophia, in whom God rejoices and delights always.[22]

For the Christian imagination, Sophia, "spread like a canopy over our sinful though still hallowed world,"[23] will find her deepest identity in Christ, who by his incarnation not only joins heaven with earth but gives humanity an honored "place" in God from the beginning. *When he established the heavens, I was there.* Like Christ and because of him every person has "a share in divine freedom and immortality."[24] In the bold formulation of St. Irenaeus, "He became human so that we might become divine." Or with Merton, "If we believe in the Incarnation of the Son of God, there should be no one on earth in whom we are not prepared to see, in mystery, the person of Christ."[25] This reaching across the threshold of eternity and history, heaven and earth, divinity and humanity, comprises the erotic structure of the whole Bible. Bulgakov thus envisions Sophia as the *eros* of God become one with creation, the love between Father, Son, and Spirit that "opens room" in God's self for creation and incarnation. As Merton proclaims, we are "saved by love, yes, even by *eros*."[26]

What is more, the Sophia tradition reaches "behind" and beyond the human world to illumine the silent grandeur of the universe itself, the "groaning" of all creation in God, the inner dynamism of matter that human beings do not simply witness but *to which* we positively belong. Immersed in prayerful communion with nature, Merton gives voice to a primordial wonder, "In me the world is present, and you are present. I am a link in the chain of light and of presence." The Wisdom tradition gives a positive language, that is, *a Name*, to an experience that resounds in persons and cultures everywhere: the intuition of nature's silent receptivity and gratuity, its beauty, mystery, and ontological depth in God—Sophia. Life itself, fundamentally, is on our side.[27]

This gathering sophianic vision of reality bursts forth in the final pages of *New Seeds of Contemplation*, where we meet the Wisdom-child of Proverbs 8, "playing in the world, playing before Him at all times."[28] "We do not have to go very far," Merton writes, "to catch echoes of that game, and of that dancing. When we are alone on a starlit night; when by chance we see the migrating birds in autumn descending on a grove of junipers to rest and eat; when we see children in a moment when they are really children; when we know love in our own hearts." All of these, "If we could let go of our own obsession with what we think is the meaning of it all," no longer would appear trivial but would strike us as invitations to "forget ourselves on purpose, cast our awful solemnity to the winds," and join in "the general dance" of Sophia, at play in the garden of the Lord.

[Wisdom] will honor you if you embrace her.
She will place on your head a fair garland;
    she will bestow on you a beautiful crown.

~ Proverbs 4:8-9 (NRSV)

Come to me, all you who labor and are
    burdened, and I will give you rest.

~ Matthew 11:28 (NABRE)

III

Dawn of Wisdom

The breakthrough of Sophia into Merton's consciousness did not simply "happen" to him all at once but was the flowering within him of years of study and meditation on the Hebrew Scriptures, patristic and Russian theology, Zen, Eastern iconography, and surely, much more than we can know, untold hours of contemplation in the hills and woods surrounding Gethsemani. In Merton, life, spirituality, and theology merge into one. From between the lines of his mystical biography, the music of her presence emerges as a kind of story-shaped Christology and mystical theology of God. Is it misguided to suggest that the contours of a single person's life may serve as a trustworthy window into the life story of God? Not in the least. In truth, the lives of the prophets, mystics, and saints reveal that this has always been the case.

As Merton writes, "Contrary to what has been thought in recent centuries in the west, the spiritual or interior life is not an exclusively private affair. . . . The spiritual life of one person is

27

simply the life of all manifesting itself in him."[1] This beautiful—
and often terrible—insight holds for Merton no less than for the
Russian writers before him. It holds for all of us. Thus, before
Sophia is or ever was an "idea" or "symbol" of God in mystical
or theological discourse, she is and has been from time imme-
morial a figure of mystical encounter in the life of God's people.
Yet she is not less than an idea or symbol either. Encounter gives
rise to image; image gives rise to thought; thought gives rise to
encounter, and again, the reaching for image and symbol. The
art and science of theology—of giving language to the revelation
of Love among God's people—is a living, breathing engagement
with the mystery of God. It therefore calls for more than a hint
of music and poetics.

For all of these reasons, I invite the reader in the following
pages to try to listen from the inside, as it were, so as to discern
something of the music or intuitive process by which Merton
comes to internalize the vision of Sophia fully as his own and
begins to communicate it with vitality in his writings—culmi-
nating in the prose poem *Hagia Sophia*, the focal point of this
and the next several conferences. From there, we shall seek after
hints of her presence rising in other places, beyond Merton's life
and beyond even an overtly Christian or religious realm. We
begin, then, with Merton's reading of the Russian theologians.

Careful readers of Merton's journals cannot help but be
struck by the degree to which Sophia's presence begins to haunt
his religious imagination during the late 1950s—thanks in
part to his close study of Russian theologians such as Bulgakov,
Berdayev, Evdokimov, and Florovsky. One of the earliest clues to

their impact on his religious imagination appears in his journal entry of April 25, 1957:

> Bulgakov and Berdyaev are writers of great, great attention. . . . These two men have dared to make mistakes and were to be condemned by every church, in order to say something great and worthy of God in the midst of all their wrong statements. They have dared to accept the challenge of the sapiential books, the challenge of the image of Proverbs where Wisdom is "playing in the world" before the face of the Creator.[2]

Merton's extensive notes on the Russian theologians convey something more than the joy and labor of fresh intellectual discovery. The Russians seem to have unlocked a door deep in Merton that had never been fully opened, at least never in such a radically personal way. Interrupting his notes, there is a sudden flash of insight and what seems the birthing of a personal creed:

> If I can unite in *myself*, in my own spiritual life, the thought of the East and the West of the Greek and Latin Fathers, I will create in myself a reunion of the divided church and from that unity in myself can come the exterior and visible unity of the church. For if we want to bring together East and West we cannot do it by imposing one upon the other. We must contain both in ourselves and transcend both in Christ.[3]

This was "a critical moment in Merton's intellectual and spiritual maturity,"[4] a revelatory moment that would spill forth vividly in the years to follow. The image of Christ as Wisdom of God, as Sophia, began to haunt Merton's religious imagination.

In the journal entry of February 28, 1958, Merton describes a hauntingly erotic dream of a young Jewish girl named "Proverb" who "clings to me and will not let go." A week later, he addresses to her a "love letter" of surprising intimacy and devotion:

> How grateful I am to you for loving in me something which I thought I had entirely lost, and someone who, I thought, I had long ago ceased to be. . . . your lovely spontaneity, your simplicity, the generosity of your love. . . . you are utterly alone: yet you have given your love to me, why I cannot imagine. . . . Dearest Proverb, I love your name, its mystery, its simplicity and its secret.[5]

To feel himself loved in such a way by *one*, it seems, had broken open Merton's capacity to love the *many*. Two weeks later, March 18, 1958, she comes to him again "in Louisville, at the corner of Fourth and Walnut," when Merton is "suddenly overwhelmed with the realization that I loved all those people, even though we were total strangers." The experience was "like waking from a dream of separateness, like news that one holds the winning ticket in a cosmic sweepstake."[6]

In a letter to the Russian novelist Boris Pasternak a few months later, Merton shares with Pasternak the experience at Fourth and Walnut, invoking the name of "Proverb" to describe the "beauty and [secret] purity" he saw reflected in the faces of the strangers passing by him on the street corner: "And they did not know their real identity as the Child so dear to God who, from before the beginning, was playing in his sight all days, playing in the world."[7] Henceforth Merton would associate her name—Wisdom, Sophia, Proverb—with the divine image alive and at play in all things, in the dance of nature and of human beings, in the pulse of Life itself unfolding. *She is in all things like the air receiving the sunlight. . . . She is the Love that unites them. She is life as communion, life as thanksgiving, life as praise, life as festival, life as glory.*[8]

Given Merton's artistic sensibilities it is not surprising that a significant "flash point" or realization of Sophia into his consciousness would come as he gazed on a work of sacred art. It happened one day in early 1959, when Merton was visiting the Viennese-born artist Victor Hammer and his wife Carolyn at their home in Lexington, Kentucky. As the three friends sat together at lunch, Merton noticed a triptych that Victor had painted, its central panel depicting the boy Christ being crowned by a dark-haired woman. As the artist would later recall, Merton, while looking at the image, "asked quite abruptly, 'And who is the woman behind Christ?' I [Victor] said, 'I do not know yet.' Without further question he [Merton] gave his own answer. 'She is Hagia Sophia, Holy Wisdom, who crowns Christ.' And this she was—and is."[9] Some days later Hammer wrote to Merton, asking him to expand on his response. Merton obliges in a letter of May 14, 1959:

> The first thing to be said, of course, is that Hagia Sophia is God Himself. God is not only a Father but a Mother. He is both at the same time. . . . To ignore this distinction

is to lose touch with the fullness of God. This is a very ancient intuition of reality which goes back to the oldest Oriental thought. . . . For the "masculine-feminine" relationship is basic in all reality—simply because all reality mirrors the reality of God.[10]

As the letter continues, Merton's thoughts seem to spill onto the page as if by stream of consciousness. His friend's inquiry seems to have unlocked a kind of floodgate in him.

Sophia, Merton explains, is "the dark, nameless *Ousia* [Being]" of God, not one of the Three Divine Persons, but each "at the same time, are Sophia and manifest her." She is "the Tao, the nameless pivot of all being and nature. . . , that which is the smallest and poorest and most humble in all." She is "the 'feminine child' playing before God the Creator in His universe, 'playing before Him at all times, playing in the world' (Proverbs 8)." Above all, Sophia is God's love and mercy coming to birth in us. "In the sense that God is Love, is Mercy, is Humility, is Hiddenness," writes Merton, "He shows Himself to us within ourselves as our own poverty . . . and if we receive the humility of God into our hearts, we become able to . . . love this very poverty, which is Himself and His Sophia." It is as if Merton is hearing again the Voice of God in Paradise, as during the "Fire Watch"—"Mercy within mercy within mercy"[11]—but now in an unmistakably feminine key: Sophia.

And then suddenly Merton speaks more directly and intimately to Victor, who had evidently shared details with him about the genesis of the painting: "The story you tell of its growth is very interesting and revealing and I am sure Hagia Sophia herself was guiding you in the process, for it is she who guides all true artists, and without her they are nothing." As he concludes the letter, Merton seems to realize that their conversation has given birth to something significant and asks Hammer: "Maybe we could make a little broadsheet on Sophia, with the material begun here???"[12] This is just what would happen.

Drawing material from the letter and his journal entries, Merton completed *Hagia Sophia* during Pentecost in the spring of 1961. Note that this is the very same Pentecost in which the "Prayer to God the Father on the Vigil of Pentecost" came to birth. It was a time of endings but also of extraordinary beginnings for Merton, the discovery and dedication of himself as an intimate "Son" and "Friend" of God: *[Here] You see me. Here You love me. Here You ask the response of my own love, and of my confidence. Here You ask me to be nothing else than Your friend.*[13] The Pentecost prayer concludes with Merton asking God for the courage to "be a man of peace and to help bring peace to the world," to learn the way "of truth and nonviolence," and for the grace to accept whatever difficult consequences might follow.

Merton was struggling to come to terms with the fact that his increasingly public stance on issues of peace and social justice would put him at odds with many Catholics, not least the leadership of his own order, who preferred the pious persona of *The Seven Storey Mountain*. "What hurts me most is to have been inexorably trapped by my own folly. Wanting to prove myself a Catholic—and of course not perfectly succeeding. They all admit and commend my good will, but frankly, I am not one of the bunch, am I?"[14] Finally, on July 23, 1961, in what seems to be a spiritual turning point, he writes: "I will stop making any kind of effort to justify myself to anybody. To prepare a place for myself anywhere, among any group. . . . Peace is impossible until I fully and totally realize, and embrace the realization, that I am already forgotten. . . . Render unto God the things that are God's."[15]

On July 2, 1960, the feast of the Visitation, Merton had recorded perhaps the most significant of all the Wisdom passages, his "awakening" by "the soft voice of the nurse" in a hospital, a passage that strangely foreshadows his encounter with Margie six years later. The experience seems to touch off in Merton not only a deep sense of gratitude and wonder—"as if the Blessed Virgin herself, as if Wisdom had awakened me"—but also of profound sorrow for the acute memory of sins past, sins which implicated him in the sufferings of the world:

> Who is more little than the helpless man, asleep in bed, having entrusted himself gladly to sleep and to night? Him the gentle voice will awake, all that is sweet in woman will awaken him. Not for conquest and pleasure, but for the far deeper wisdom of love and joy and communion.
>
> My heart is broken for all my sins and the sins of the whole world, for the rottenness of our spirit of gain that defiles wisdom in all beings—to rob and deflower wisdom as if there were only a little pleasure to be had, only a little joy, and it had to be stolen, violently taken and spoiled. When all the while her warmth, her exuberant silence, her acceptance, are infinite, infinite! Deep is the ocean, boundless sweetness, kindness, humility, silence

of wisdom that is not abstract, disconnected, fleshless. Awakening us gently when we have exhausted ourselves to night and to sleep. O Dawn of Wisdom![16]

Here Merton has fully internalized one of the more striking insights at the heart of the Russian Wisdom tradition, namely, that "Continence toward woman and reverence for creation are intimately connected."[17] To say it more bluntly, Merton here links the wholesale objectification of women and women's *bodies* in society with the objectification and destruction of the *natural world*: Sophia, the "Mother" who bears and sustains life; Sophia, the "Lover" whose beauty and physical touch landscapes our basic sense of "being at home" in the cosmos.

At the end of a retreat in January 1961, just a few months before composing *Hagia Sophia*, Merton is gripped again by Sophia's presence in the writings of Russian theologian Paul Evdokimov:

> Long quiet intervals in dark hours. Evdokimov on orthodoxy—once again, as I have so many times recently, I need the concept of *natura naturans* [nature acting according to its nature]—the divine wisdom in ideal nature, the ikon of wisdom, the dancing ikon—the summit reached by so many non-Christian contemplatives (would that it were reached by a few Christians!) Summit of Vedanta?—
>
> Faith in Sophia, *natura naturans*, the great stabilizer today—for peace.
>
> The basic hope that people have that man will somehow not be completely destroyed is hope in *natura naturans*.
>
> —The dark face, the "night face" of Sophia—pain, trouble, pestilence.[18]

Here is another passage worthy of slow rumination. In his book *The Feminine and the Salvation of the World*, Evdokimov had written: "An icon is a theology in lines and colors, a true *locus theologicus*, one of the most expressive elements of the Tradition. . . . It is a sacrament, not of divine action, but of a divine presence. . . . It makes the invisible visible to 'the eyes of the mind.'"[19] In Orthodox spirituality, the act of praying before an icon draws us into the real presence of the saint, Christ, Mary, or, in Merton's case, gazing on Hammer's image of Holy Wisdom, God revealed as Sancta Sophia.[20] Note how Merton links the divine "presence" experienced in prayer before icons with the "summit reached by so many non-Christian contemplatives," suggesting that the wordless communion shared by contemplatives of different religious traditions has to do with making "the invisible visible to 'the eyes of the mind.'" But there is also this: years of meditation on the Wisdom tradition had brought Merton here to the rather striking insight that faith in Sophia is "the great stabilizer today for peace"—an intuition that would find its most sublime voice in *Hagia Sophia*.

For Merton and the Russian theologians, to invoke Sophia's name is to remember both the Name of God and our own deepest identity. It is to place oneself in God's presence—"I am with you, here, now, in the present moment"—to open oneself to God's energy, and to offer oneself as an instrument and a living sacrifice in God's hands. Her name tells us nothing essentially "new" but awakens a union that already exists, always and everywhere, even if it is far, tragically far, from being realized. And that is why her name is disruptive, uncomfortable, dangerous—

awakening deep memory, disturbing conscience, provoking response. "It is like all minds coming back together into awareness from all distractions, cross-purposes and confusions, into unity of love."[21]

Is this not the *very same mind* that was awakening in Gandhi and King: "a mind of love, of understanding, of infinite capaciousness"? Is she not the same divine Child who sleeps and hides in all the people, whose secret innocence "opens the door to a life in which the individual is not lost in the cosmos and in society but found in them"? Is hers not the same Spirit who summons the freedom for creativity, love, and mercy that we share with our brother and savior Jesus Christ, by whose incarnation all life is made "sacred and meaningful—even that which [we have come] to call secular and profane"?[22] But then, what are we to make of Merton's gesture here to the "dark face," the "night face" of Sophia—Sophia *bound up* in "pain, trouble, pestilence"?

In January 1962, *Hagia Sophia* came to print in a stunning limited edition on Victor Hammer's hand press, with Hammer's icon illustrating the text. It would finally become the centerpiece of *Emblems of a Season of Fury*, published in the same year. The prominent placement of *Hagia Sophia* in this collection, which includes devastating poems on racism ("And the Children of Birmingham"), genocide ("Chant to Be Used in Processions around a Site with Furnaces"), and political oppression ("A Picture of Lee Ying"), calls to mind the journal entry of January 26, 1961: "Faith in Sophia, *natura naturans*, the great stabilizer today—for peace." It seems that God had responded generously to Merton's prayer for courage and would do so to the end of his life. In *Hagia*

Sophia, Merton not only anticipates the concerns of feminist and environmentalist theologies; he gives us "an elemental model on the birthing of peace." [23]

The image of "birthing," finally, is apt. As I hinted at the beginning of this conference, no less significant than the theological implications we might draw from Merton's awakening to Sophia is the process itself of realization in Merton, in us, in the whole human community—the dynamics of breakthrough and struggle and ecstasy that mark our growing into the truth about the mystery of God. Indeed, the constellation of events by which *Hagia Sophia* comes to birth in Merton can teach us something beautiful about how God works in each of us: by invitation and by stealth, if you will, never by coercion, drawing us with mercy and patience toward the way of peace, truth, and nonviolence.

"There lives the dearest freshness deep down things," [24] writes the Jesuit poet Gerard Manley Hopkins. The image gives rise to a beautiful but perilous thought. *Grace builds on nature.* Human beings—through "God's Art and Incarnation" in each of us—must learn to discover and labor with God in and through *found materials*, in the ordinary and extraordinary stuff of our own lives. "It is she who guides all true artists," as Merton tells his friend, "and without her they are nothing." But with her the artist comes alive in each of us. Not least, we are called to work in harmony with the beautiful, suffering Earth and all its creatures. Like Merton, we must learn to read the signs of our times with penetration. [25]

Christ unrolls the
meaning of the
old Testament

IV

From End to End Mightily

he best grasp of mystical texts, as Mark Burrows reminds us, comes "not in criticism of the text, but in the 'performance' of reading, that moment when the mystical text becomes the occasion for a 'merging of the way of knowledge and the way of love.'"[1] If *Hagia Sophia* is anything, it is just such a mystical text, a realization of knowledge and love which came to slow birth in Merton but which now awaits gestation in readers willing to give themselves over to its play of images and silences. For this reason, before reading further, I encourage the reader to linger in the text of *Hagia Sophia* for a while, or, even better, to read it aloud in a contemplative setting with others.[2] What emerges in such readings is no less potentially valid or fruitful than insights drawn from sustained critical-intellectual analysis. Here I want to reflect on the third and the fourth (final) sections of *Hagia Sophia*: "III. High Morning: The Hour of Tierce" and "IV. Sunset: The Hour of Compline; *Salve Regina*."

At High Morning the Sun as the "Face of God" is "diffused" mercifully into the softer light of Hagia Sophia, who shines not *on* all things so much as *from within them*, speaking "to us gently in ten thousand things." The image recalls Hopkins's "As Kingfishers Catch Fire": *For Christ plays in ten thousand places / Lovely in limbs, and lovely in lives not his.*[3] The section proceeds in layers of rich imagery, reprising themes from Merton's effusive letter on Hagia Sophia to his friend Victor Hammer:

> All the perfections of created things are also in God; and therefore He is at once Father and Mother. As Father He stands in solitary might surrounded by darkness. As Mother His shining is diffused, embracing all His creatures with merciful tenderness and light. The Diffuse Shining of God is Hagia Sophia. We call her His "glory." In Sophia His power is experienced only as mercy and as love.[4]

Lyrical passages of naming and unnaming follow, marking the hour of High Morning with palpable wonder and mystery. The speaker has experienced something extraordinary and cannot be silent yet struggles to say exactly what or who Sophia is. "Perhaps in a certain very primitive aspect Sophia is the unknown, the dark, the nameless Ousia. Perhaps she is even the Divine Nature, One in Father, Son and Holy Ghost. . . . This I do not know. Out of the silence Light is spoken." Biblical *memoria* rises to the surface, as diffuse light is sought out in primordial darkness, "In the Nameless Beginning, without Beginning." Most striking in this section is the oxymoronic coincidence of male and female metaphors, light and darkness, theophany and hiddenness. As poet Susan McCaslin observes, "The efforts to name Sophia, to catch her in the net of language defer to the apophatic tradition of 'unnaming.' Every naming becomes an unnaming, a backing off from language, and an insistence that words and names are inadequate before mystery. Sophia herself becomes 'the unknown, the dark, the nameless.'" The dance back and forth between naming and unnaming reminds us that "God is not an object of knowledge. The God who is male and female, father and mother, is simultaneously neither male nor female, transcending gender categories."[5]

But then there is a sudden shift in tone, a new confidence and seeming clarity: "Now the Wisdom of God, Sophia, comes forth, reaching from 'end to end mightily.'" She wills to be "the unseen pivot of all nature," "that which is poorest and humblest, that which is hidden in all things," yet also that which is "quite manifest, for it is their own self that stands before us, naked and without care." She is the feminine Child "playing in the world, obvious and unseen, playing at all times before the Creator," who "wills to be with the children of men. She is their sister. . . . She is God-given and God Himself as Gift."

While a feminist reading of the poem could find problematic "the identification of the feminine with mercy and tenderness," in fact, as McCaslin notes, there is no hierarchical "subordination of Sophia to a masculine God."[6] Qualities of tenderness and mercy are also attributed to God the Father, just as Sophia exercises power and authority throughout the poem, as when she crowns the Logos and sends him forth into the world in section IV. In short, gender metaphors are "interconnected and interchangeable," "an expression of two aspects of a single dynamic at play, like Wisdom at the foundation of the world."[7] Merton's metaphors remain fluid. Sophia "is not just the feminine face of a masculine God, or a masculine God with feminine attributes (God in a skirt), but an active power permeating all things."[8]

And yet for me what makes this section of *Hagia Sophia* so striking is not only its apophatic dance of saying and unsaying—that is, the tension McCaslin describes between "X" and "not-X" that traditionally characterizes mystical texts—but even more its cumulative layering of positive images for the divine in the pattern of "X" and "Y" and "Z" and "A" and "B" and "C." By juxtaposing images long separated in the Christian imagination, only rarely emerging in conjunction—"Jesus our mother" (from Julian of Norwich); "He is Father and Mother"; "We call her His 'glory'"; "She is the Bride and the Feast and the Wedding"— Merton carries us beyond the dialectic of positive/negative theology into a kind of mystical third moment, where idols are shattered not in the silence of negation but in the plenitude of affirmation, unity-in-difference, and ecstatic praise. In short, Merton ushers us into a mosaic experience of God brimming with positive content, spilling over its linguistic containers.[9]

The last part of section III considers the wonder of Sophia's reception in the world of creatures. Though the fallen world prefers darkness to light, she is nevertheless received by many and is the secret wellspring of beauty, creativity, and tenderness: "All things praise her by being themselves and by sharing in the Wedding Feast. She is the Bride and the Feast and the Wedding." The notion of all things giving glory to God simply by "being themselves" echoes a classic theme of transcendental Thomism and calls to mind one of Merton's most celebrated texts, "Things in Their Identity," which opens simply, and unforgettably: "A tree gives glory to God by being a tree."[10]

Yet the "softer light" of Hagia Sophia casts the veil joining heaven and earth in a *particular kind of radiance*, which "would almost seem to be, in herself, all mercy." Sophia is "the mercy of God in us," the power of pardon which "turns the darkness of our sins into the light of grace." Indeed, as mercy "she does in us a greater work than that of Creation: the work of new being in grace, the work of pardon, the work of transformation." Echoing the Wisdom literature of the Bible and St. Paul's theology of adoption in Christ, the poem here ascribes to human beings a particular place of honor and responsibility in creation, an honor that bears with it, however, a perilous kenotic sting.

To recall Merton's prayer for courage on the Vigil of Pentecost, as daughters, sons, and "friends" of God, each of us are called by name "to help bring peace to the world," to learn the way "of truth and nonviolence," and to bear freely the consequences that follow. The third part of the poem thus leads to the need for the incarnation, the focus of the final section, where Mary and her "fiat" take center stage as exemplary of God's summons to human freedom, our "yes," which opens the way for the birth of Love in the world.[11]

It is she, it is Mary, Sophia, who in sadness and joy, with the full awareness of what she is doing, sets upon the Second Person, the Logos, a crown which is His Human Nature. Thus her consent opens the door of created nature, of time, of history, to the Word of God.

God enters into His creation. Through her wise answer, through her obedient understanding, through the

sweet yielding consent of Sophia, God enters without
publicity into the city of rapacious men.[12]

Of course, the freedom for love also implies the freedom to *refuse*
Sophia's invitation. Thus she stands in the delicate boundary
between freedom and grace.

On this point it is worth pausing to contemplate Merton's
mysterious ink drawing, "Christ Unveils the Meaning of the Old
Testament," which graces the cover of this book. In her penetrating study of the image, Margaret Bridget Betz describes it as
expressive of "Merton's intuitive grasp of a God more inclusive
than the traditional patriarchal God, and, like the God of the
Psalms, all-encompassing."[13] Can somebody say Amen?! I don't
wish to add much more than this, except to underscore that for
Merton it is *Christ* who unveils Sophia, the divine power realized
in human beings as Love and Mercy. And yet, gazing further, one
might suggest that even as Sophia is unveiled and known by all,
Christ willingly recedes into the background. Why? Because, as
the disciples discovered on the way to Emmaus, as Merton wrote
to Suzuki, "We follow him, we find him, and then we must go
our way without him."[14] As we live and grow in Christ through
the power of the Holy Spirit, he/she/God comes to birth *in us*.
"Because He is even closer than that. He is *ourself.*"

Thus in Merton's drawing it is Hebrew Wisdom, she that
is "older," paradoxically, who stands youthful and vibrant in the
foreground—reversing the more traditional arrangement of the
male and female figures in Victor Hammer's "Hagia Sophia."
She is at once wordlessly Ancient ("When he established the
heavens, I was there") and unabashedly New, a Child full of

promise and possibility, ready to play in the world, "like the air receiving the sunlight." Just as Mary in *Hagia Sophia* "opens the way" for Christ with "full awareness of what she is doing," so Christ in Merton's drawing, in the fullness of time and with full awareness of what he is doing, opens the way for Sophia, the birthing of love and peace in each of us, in all of God's children. Merton's spirituality thus moves through one center, who is Christ Jesus, unveiling Sophia, the hidden Heart of Love.[15] Pressing further, we might even discern in Merton's image the mysterious movement of the Holy Spirit in *the act itself* of unveiling, of unbinding, of unsilencing and setting free Sophia.

She is the divine Child who sleeps in all the people. She is the Love in God that unites the people, always and everywhere—Christians and Jews, Muslims and Hindus, Buddhists and Seekers, believers and atheists. The Love of God unveiled in Christ Jesus by the power of the Holy Spirit knows no bounds (Gal 3:28). Merton's drawing celebrates, if obscurely, the *wholeness* of God, the integral fullness of the *imago Dei*, male and female, realized (made real) wherever human beings seek to be and become Love in the rough and beautiful tumble of their ordinary lives. "Gentleness comes to him when he is most helpless and awakens him, refreshed, beginning to be made whole. Love takes him by the hand, and opens to him the door to another life, another day."

The final scene of *Hagia Sophia* is a scene of great beauty and piercing loneliness, the image of a God who shares freely without reserve the poverty, and glory, of our human condition.[16]

> The shadows fall. The stars appear. The birds begin to sleep. Night embraces the silent half of the earth.

A vagrant, a destitute wanderer with dusty feet, finds his way down a new road. A homeless God, lost in the night, without papers, without identification, without even a number, a frail expendable exile lies down in desolation under the sweet stars of the world and entrusts Himself to sleep.

V

The Night Face of Sophia

"[The] night has values that the day never dreamed of," Merton had written in "Fire Watch: July 4, 1952." More than a decade later, in the deep winter of 1965, Merton penned two passages in his journal that I want to explore here for the way they illuminate "through a glass darkly," as it were, the mysterious and beautiful ways that Sophia moves and rises in Merton's consciousness as he responds to the world around him. The first passage Merton wrote on his fiftieth birthday, January 31, 1965, opening his journal on the auspicious occasion by citing from Wisdom 8:16: *Intrans in domum meam, conquiescam cum illa: non enim habet amaritudinem conversatio illius, sed laetitiam et gaudium* ["When I go home I shall take my ease with her, for nothing is bitter in her company, when life is shared with her there is no pain, nothing but pleasure and joy"].[1] Though he complains of suffering bitterly from the "fierce cold all night, certainly down to zero," Merton expresses joy in the fact that "I woke up in a hermitage!" Hearkening then to the Wisdom text, Merton wonders:

But what more do I seek than this silence, this simplicity, this "living together with wisdom?" For me there is nothing else. . . . I have nothing to justify and nothing to defend: I need only defend this vast simple emptiness from my own self, and the rest is clear. (Through the cold and darkness I hear the angelus ringing at the monastery.) The beautiful jeweled shining of honey in the lamplight. Festival![2]

There follows immediately a "thought that came to me during meditation." The thought turns out to be a devastating indictment of racism, and the dehumanization of persons generally, which Merton sees poisoning the atmosphere of modern mass society.

The error of racism is the logical consequence of an essentialist style of thought. Finding out what a man is and then nailing him to a definition so that there can be no change. A White Man is a White Man, and that is it. A Negro, even though he is three parts white is "A Negro" with all that our rigid definition predicates of a Negro. And so the logical machine can devour him because of his essence. Do you think that in an era of existentialism this will get better? On the contrary: definitions, more and more schematic, are fed into computers. The machines are meditating on the most arbitrary and rudimentary of essences, punched into IBM cards, and defining you and me forever without appeal. "A priest," "A Negro," "A Jew," "A Socialist," etc.[3]

The striking juxtaposition of the "Festival!" flashing off an ordinary honey jar in the lamplight with the specter of wholesale racism, exploding in cities across America in 1965, illustrates almost perfectly the dynamic of Merton's thinking *and* praying throughout the tumultuous decade. To "live together with wisdom" is to live fully awake in the center of these contradictions of our times yet refuse to be *defined* by them, like an "essence" fed into a computer. For when I am "home with her" I can "take my ease," for nothing is bitter in her company.

But there is a second remarkable passage to consider, coming just four days (February 4, 1965) after Merton had lamented "all that our rigid definition predicates of a Negro":

> Last night I had a curious and moving dream about a "Black Mother." I was in a place (where? Somewhere I had been as a child, but there also seemed to be some connection with the valley over at Edelin's) and I realized that I had come there for a reunion with a Negro foster mother whom I had loved in my childhood. Indeed, I owed, it seemed, my life to her love so that it was she really, and not my natural mother, who had given me life. As if from her hand had come a new *life* and there she was. Her face was ugly and severe, yet a great warmth came from her to me, and we embraced with great love (and I with much gratitude). What I recognized was not her face but *the warmth of her embrace and of her heart*, so to speak. We danced a little together, I and my Black Mother, and then I had to continue the journey I was on. I cannot remember more about this journey and many incidents connected with it. Comings and goings, and turning back, etc.[4]

What Merton "recognized" in this dream, it seems to me, was the very same "presence" he strived to recognize in everyone: "the warmth of her embrace and of her heart." No matter that "her face was ugly and severe," what moves Merton is that "a great warmth came from her to me," "as if from her hand had come a new *life*." Notice how Merton experiences himself as the object of Wisdom's intimate attention; her embrace is *transitive*, so to speak, breaking in "from her to me" yet coming in the form of this concrete person or thing before him right now: the flight of an escaping dove; a lone deer feeding among the trees outside the hermitage; the faces of passersby on a busy street corner. For she *is playing in the world, obvious and unseen, playing at all times before the Creator*.[5]

I want to linger a moment longer on the darker notes of lament and protest in these passages. On the one hand, as intimated in the previous conference, Sophia moves through the world with creative power and grace, reaching "from end to end mightily" and breaking into human consciousness "with a liberty that knows no law of man"; on the other, she appears constrained and disfigured, *imprisoned* by the fallenness of human freedom, as Merton puts it, by "the rottenness of our spirit of gain that defiles wisdom in all beings." The warmth and transcendent beauty of Merton's "Black Mother," for example, is unseen by all but a few because of "all that our rigid definition predicates of a Negro." Because she is known by the world as "Negro" before she is a *person*, a beautiful daughter of God, "the logical machine can devour [her] because of [her] essence."

Thus in his dreams no less than his waking hours Merton confronts "the dark face, the 'night face' of Sophia," the Child bound and disfigured by "the world of rapacious men." She is the "homeless God" in the final scene of *Hagia Sophia*, "lost in the night, without papers, without identification, without even a number." She is Christ our brother, who is still crucified, disfigured, and silenced in people everywhere, and in the suffering Earth. No less than in Christ, her suffering in people today is "not abstract, disconnected, fleshless," but it is real, often horribly real—*as if there were only a little pleasure to be had, only a little joy, and it had to be stolen, violently taken and spoiled. When all the while her warmth, her exuberant silence, her acceptance, are infinite, infinite!*

If there is a coda to this sequence of Wisdom encounters it comes in Merton's relationship with "M," the student nurse with whom he fell in love in 1966—the "deep, mysterious, personal, unique" woman "in the depths of my heart [who] *is not symbolic*," who "is trying to become free in my love and is clinging to me for love and help."[6] With her love and help Merton would discover for perhaps the first time the freedom of loving a woman "not for conquest and pleasure, but for the far deeper wisdom of love and joy and communion." Following an affectionate phone call with M. from a phone booth near Bardstown (September 10, 1966), Merton struggles to reconcile all of these "strange connections" with the feminine, this "secret child" in his "deepest heart":

> I forgot to ask the exact date of M.'s birthday. (She was born just about two months before I came through Cincinnati on my way to Gethsemani! I had walked through Cincinnati station with the words of Proverbs 8 in my mind: "And my delights were to be with the children of men!"—I have never forgotten this, it struck me forcibly

then! Strange connection in my deepest heart—between
M. and the "Wisdom" figure—and Mary—and the Feminine in the Bible—Eve, etc.—Paradise—Most mysterious,
haunting, deep, lovely, moving, transforming!)[7]

When the relationship had finally been "amputated just when
it was about to begin," and done so by Merton, he struggled to
reconcile the contradictions of their situation, "the awful loneliness, deprivation, desolation of being without each other, even
though in our hearts we continue to love each other deeply."[8]
On the one hand, "it is merely what I have chosen and the choice
is ratified over and over each day"; on the other, "I so vividly
remember her body and long for her love."[9] The real coda was
surely yet to come, in the rupture and cost of an altogether new
and now more ambiguous commitment to chastity and solitude
on the other side of such a love.

> I cannot regard this as "just an episode." It is a profound
> event in my life and one which will have entered deeply
> into my heart to alter and transform my whole climate
> of thought and experience: for in her I now realize I had
> found something, someone, that I had been looking for all
> my life. I know too that she feels the same about me. . . .
> I think we will both always feel that this was and is some-
> thing too deep and too real to be essentially changed.[10]

By way of summary, let me offer two observations with re-
spect to Merton's encounters with Sophia during the last decade
of his life. First, by the turn of the 1960s, the "Festival!" of life—
the *whole* of it—had become of one piece for Merton. Merton

refused to separate mysticism from politics or any other area of human life. In this sense Sophia, like his beloved "M.," is *not symbolic* but she is real, more than literally real. In his dance with the living God Merton shows himself to be an integral and embodied human being like the rest of us—not least all who have come to know God's nearness and grace through the mystery of erotic love. Second, the journals bring us "face-to-face" with the central dynamic of Merton's person-centered spirituality, his sense of God not only as the all-embracing "hidden ground of Love" but also as personal Presence, who holds us in *the warmth of her embrace and of her heart.*

Merton had come to believe—that is, to experience and trust—that at the base of all reality is the wisdom of Love, Sophia, a wisdom which deepens whenever we truly love another person. By our love we can unite ourselves to one another, even the stranger and enemy, in the very life of God. While utterly free, gratuitous, and unexpected—"As if from her hand had come a new *life*"—Wisdom's embrace is also felt as a remembering, an awakening from sleep, a kind of homecoming or rediscovery of one's true self held in the loving mercy of God. Once Merton *woke up*, that is, once he surrendered to this merciful love *for himself*, he could no longer regard any encounter with the world as "just an episode." At home in her presence, the world had become for him an epiphany of God.

It is important to reiterate that there was nothing abstract or esoteric for Merton about the encounter with divine Sophia: "It is simply opening yourself to receive. The presence of God is like walking out of a door into the fresh air. You don't concentrate on the fresh air, you breathe it. And you don't concentrate on the sunlight, you just enjoy it. It is all around."[11] She comes to us not through the embrace of an elaborate theology but in the music of life itself, when we respond to life's invitation to be truly awake and to live. More than this, our response to God's freedom for Love *moves both ways*, as it were, with our acts of compassion and creativity reverberating back into the very Being of God. God—the so-called Unmoved Mover—is moved and transformed by our acts of love. With the coming of Christ "the reign of numbers" has come to an end. "Individual human life became the life story of God and its contents filled the vast expanses of the universe."[12]

From his first encounters with Sophia in the late 1950s to the day of his sudden death in Bangkok in 1968, Merton lived as a man possessed by the conviction that "one can seek to discover and will discover that 'God is all in all.'"[13]

> For she is the refulgence of eternal light,
>   the spotless mirror of the power of God,
>   the image of his goodness. . . .
> And passing into holy souls from age to age,
>   she produces friends of God and prophets.
>
>   (Wis 7:26-27; NAB)

The stars rejoice in their setting, and in the rising of the Sun. The heavenly lights rejoice in the going forth of one man to make a new world in the morning, because he has come out of the confused primordial dark night into consciousness. He has expressed the clear silence of Sophia in his own heart. He has become eternal.[14]

[His] rebellion is the rebellion of life against inertia, of mercy and love against tyranny, of humanity against cruelty and arbitrary violence. And he calls upon the feminine, the wordless, the timelessly moving elements to witness his sufferings. Earth hears him.

> ~ Thomas Merton, "Prometheus:
> A Meditation"

Sometimes when I stand in some corner of the camp, my feet planted on earth, my eyes raised towards heaven, tears run down my face, tears of deep emotion and gratitude.

> ~ Etty Hillesum,
> *Letters from Westerbork*, 1942

A world without mercy is not a human world.

> ~ Cardinal Walter Kasper

VI

Bearer of Hope

To this point I have tried to illumine Merton's remembrance of Wisdom-Sophia as a piece of a much broader human struggle during the twentieth century. Like his prophetic contemporaries—Gandhi, Heschel, Bonhoeffer, Day, King—Merton saw the world's social ills as symptoms of a deep and pervasive spiritual crisis. Indeed, for Merton and the Russian mystical theologians who so captured his attention, the breakthrough of Sophia corresponds with the crisis of hope in the human community, a seeming hopelessness in the face of systemic evil and senseless suffering on a scale beyond comprehension. Wisdom emerges in Merton's corpus as both a signal of (quiet) protest and at once a profound affirmation of God's undying (and dying) presence to a stricken world.[1]

Yet if faith in Sophia is "the great stabilizer today" for peace, then why do so few seem to know her? If Wisdom is the very Being or Love of God poured out in all and through all things, why do we so often fail to perceive her, and with such terrible consequences? In their "daring" interpretation of biblical Wisdom, in their poetry and dreams of Sophia, is it possible that Merton and his Russian forebears were *merely dreaming*? What about the sheer scope of evil and innocent suffering in the world, the massive destructiveness of human freedom—"the dark face, the 'night face' of Sophia—pain, trouble, pestilence"?[2] At stake here is the question of God's relationship to human history in the face of apparent hopelessness, which is also the question of credibility. What reasons can we give for the hope that is in us? Is our faith trustworthy?

I want to begin a response to this question with a brief remembrance of Fr. Alfred Delp, a Jesuit priest who was executed on February 2, 1945, for his resistance to Nazism. In a letter to his friends from prison, Fr. Delp wrote about the beauty and the cost of a life lived ever more freely under the horizon of grace. If we keep in mind the anguishing context in which these words were written, the following passage intensifies all the more our theme of hope and its relation to Wisdom:

> One thing is clear and tangible to me in a way that it seldom has been: the world is full of God. From every pore, God rushes out to us, as it were. But we're often blind. We remain stuck in the good times and the bad times and don't experience them right up to the point where the spring flows from God. . . . In everything, God wants to celebrate encounter and asks for the prayerful response of surrender. The trick and the duty is only this: to develop a lasting awareness and a lasting attitude out of these insights and graces—or rather, to allow them to develop. Then life becomes free, in that freedom which we have often looked for.[3]

The witness of mystics, sages, and ordinary people of faith down through the ages suggests that rising up from within creation there pulses an uncontainable Love, coming toward us in all things. Indeed, their witness says to us, "God rushes out to us from every pore." But can we believe it? This, I think, is Merton's particular gift: he helps us to believe it, that God is everywhere and desires in all things to be known. Or better, Merton helps us to *feel* it, and therefore to feel hope, which is the capacity to imagine again. Here is my thesis: Hope in the key of Wisdom awakens "that freedom which we have often looked for," drawing us into the future, the future of God's own imagining.

> At five-thirty in the morning I am dreaming in a very quiet room when a soft voice awakens me from my dream. I am like all mankind awakening from all the dreams that ever were dreamed in all the nights of the world. It is like the One Christ awakening in all the separate selves that ever were separate and isolated and alone in all the lands of the earth. It is like all minds coming back together into awareness from all distractions, cross-purposes and confusions, into unity of love. It is like the first morning of the world (when Adam, at the sweet voice of Wisdom awoke from nonentity and knew her), and like the Last Morning of the world when all the fragments of Adam will return from death at the voice of Hagia Sophia, and will know where they stand.[4]

Merton helps us to see—that is, to *feel in our whole person*—that while the world is stricken deeply by sin, it is also limned in the light of resurrection. Death is neither the first nor the last word.

The lure of Wisdom-Sophia throughout Merton's corpus is just this, a *lure*, if we can adopt for a moment the fish's perspective. You see the lure flashing and dancing and singing in the waters just out in front of you, inviting and drawing you forward: she is God's call from the future breaking ever into the present. And just when you think you've got her, lunging forward and capturing her in your teeth, you find that it is you who have been gotten by her; she captures you, your whole self, and will not let you go. We style ourselves as the one pursuing and discover with a jolt that it is she, God herself, who initiates and sustains the pursuit from the very beginning. She is the Love of love itself in the Heart of God, spilling over into the creativity of life unfolding over deep, deep time. Perhaps she is more like the water itself that bears and animates both fish and lure, not *that which* we see but that *through which* we see—the veil of Love and Light enlivening. And still she dances and sings before us, shining from within all things, refusing to be domesticated.

In an earlier conference I called Merton an artist, but here I qualify: it is God the Artist, the Gift of the Creator's thought and Art who speaks in and through him in the poem *Hagia Sophia*. Merton is like the poet Lurii whom he celebrates in Pasternak's novel, *Dr. Zhivago*, the poet who "felt that the main part of the work was being done not by him but by a superior power that was above him and directed him. . . . And he felt himself to be only the occasion, the fulcrum, needed to make this movement possible."[5] For me and for countless others, Merton's writings have been a kind of "fulcrum," making a little more possible in our lives the movement of spirit between heaven and earth, matter and spirit, freedom and grace.

Rowan Williams, the former archbishop of Canterbury and a sensitive poet and theologian in his own right, reinforces this point, if rather more provocatively, when he likens Merton at his best to "the poverty of the priest who vanishes into the Mass."[6]

> Merton's genius was largely that he was a massively unoriginal man: he is extraordinary because he is so dramatically absorbed by every environment he finds himself in—America between the wars, classical pre-conciliar Catholicism and monasticism, the peace movement, Asia. In all these contexts he is utterly "priestly" because he is utterly *attentive*: he does not organize, dominate, or even interpret, much of the time, but responds . . . [and] all these influences flow in to one constant place, a will and imagination turned Godward.[7]

These are points really worth pondering! Who would ever think to describe Merton as a "massively unoriginal man"? What is Williams driving at here?

"The great Christian," he continues, "is the man or woman who can make me more interested in God than in him or her." Merton is a great Christian because he "will not *let* me look at him for long: he will, finally, persuade me to look in the direction he is looking," toward a world everywhere haunted by God. "I don't want to know much more about Merton," Williams confesses. "He is dead, and I shall commend him regularly, lovingly, and thankfully to God. I am concerned to find how I can turn further in the direction he is looking, in prayer, poetry, theology, and encounter with the experience of other faiths; in trust and love of God our savior."[8] For all the fascination and inspiration

Merton's life story has been to me, I basically agree with Rowan Williams: "being interested in Thomas Merton is not being interested in an original, a 'shaping' mind, but being interested in God and human possibilities."[9]

Thus, for me, the question of Wisdom-Sophia in Merton's life is not primarily a psychological question, though it is surely that; nor is it a strictly literary and poetic question, though it is certainly that. At its core it is the question of God, which many others of his time were asking, and which people today are asking with great urgency. Where is God? Who is God? Or simply, *Is* God? And if God is, then why is the world in such a damn mess? More precisely, how do we distinguish the true God, the One who is real and trustworthy, from the idols of death of our time?[10]

In her luminous reading of *Hagia Sophia*, Susan McCaslin observes that Merton was aware that the Wisdom-Sophia tradition "had been marginalized within Western Christianity," and with *Hagia Sophia* he "attempts to restore it."[11] This much to me is clear and quite significant. Merton sought to retrieve a memory and experience of God largely lost in the Christian West, and at great price. Yet for me an even more significant assertion follows: "While Merton recognizes the limitations of language," McCaslin writes, "he assumes a metaphysical and ontological ground of being beyond language; that is, the 'real presence' of Wisdom behind and within the signs."[12] What can it mean to affirm "the real presence" of Wisdom behind and within the signs?

When Jesus of Nazareth prefaced his enigmatic sayings with the words, "let those with eyes to see and ears to hear," scholars tell us he was speaking as a teacher of Jewish wisdom, appealing not just to the head but to the whole person of his listener: heart, body, mind, senses, imagination.[13] Like a lure, his words dance before the imagination, breaking open our habitual assumptions about God and *the way things are*. This too is Merton's gift, but it is not necessarily an easy or pleasant gift to receive, neither from Jesus nor from Merton. To be "born again" is to break free of the stultifying womb of conventional human wisdom. It is to risk the vulnerability of a faith that holds no guarantees: listen to the silence, hear the forgotten histories, let the music of things unseen and hidden speak to you, jolt you from your slumber. Nothing is impossible with God. Can you believe it?

Now the Wisdom of God, Sophia, comes forth, reaching from "end to end mightily." She wills to be also the unseen pivot of all nature, the center and significance of all the light that is in all and for all. . . . But she remains unseen, glimpsed only by a few. Sometimes there are none who know her at all.[14]

The imagination that bears hope, hope in the key of Wisdom, sees promise rising in life itself and in life's protest, the sacred longing for life and communion that pulses in the very substance of things, beckoning freedom forward, daring us to imagine and make room for another possible future. By contrast, the imagination that produces despair and world-weary cynicism is like a tightening barbed-wire circle, a series of closing doors that promise nothing new but only more of the same, the same horizontal flight across the dull surface of history. Despair cannot see beyond or imagine a way out. It infuses life with a dread weariness.[15] And still she dances before us, *Sophia, the feminine child, is playing in the world, obvious and unseen, playing at all times before the Creator.*

All of this is to suggest that Merton is not just painting pretty pictures in *Hagia Sophia*. Immersed body and soul in the tradition, he writes as a mystical theologian, a poet of the presence of God. His task is not to defend a traditional understanding of God but to articulate a mode of divine presence responsive to the crisis of his times, a mode of presence faithful to the revelation of God and humanity fully alive in Jesus, but if real and authentic, a mode of presence, a kind of God-talk (that is, a theology), that will resonate in a key familiar to others both within and beyond Christianity and the Catholic Church. To grasp the "real presence" of Wisdom implies no magic, literary or otherwise. It does imply that we, like Merton, have to learn to read the signs of our times, patiently and prayerfully, with penetration. It is to learn with constant humility "the freedom of God at work outside of all set forms, all rites, all theology, all contemplation—everything." [16]

In the next conference we shall leave Merton behind for a time and embark on a kind of experiment in sophianic imagination. In the spirit of Rowan Williams's call to turn "further in the direction [Merton] is looking," we shall chase after the lure of Sophia in other places, particularly in the Jewish community, a community of critical importance to Merton in the last decade of his life. Of course, the memory of the Jewish people during the twentieth century is painfully replete with the problem of God. Where was God through these unspeakably dark passages? We will begin with the witness of a young Jewish woman named Etty

Hillesum whose story intensifies the question of God during the Holocaust. Her story and the witness of other women like her compel us to ask not only "where" and "why" but, perhaps just as significantly, *who* was God, during the Shoah?

VII

She Cannot Be a Prisoner

*E*tty Hillesum was a Dutch Jew who lived in Amsterdam during the Nazi occupation and was murdered in Auschwitz at the age of twenty-nine. Her diaries, which survived the war, give witness to a spirit in humanity that defies rational explanation. In May of 1942, just before Etty was arrested and sent to the transit camp of Westerbork, she wrote the following passage in her diary, lines that have haunted me since I first read them some twenty-five years ago:

> *Saturday morning, 7:30.* The bare trunks that climb past my window now shelter under a cover of young green leaves. A springy fleece along their naked, tough, ascetic limbs.
>
> I went to bed early last night, and from my bed I stared out through the large open window. And it was once more as if life with all its mysteries was close to me, as if I could touch it. I had the feeling that I was resting against the naked breast of life, and could feel her gentle and regular heartbeat. I felt safe and protected. And I thought, How

71

strange. It is wartime. There are concentration camps. . . .
I know how very nervous people are, I know about the
mounting human suffering. I know the persecution and
oppression and despotism and the impotent fury and the
terrible sadism. I know it all.

And yet—at unguarded moments, when left to myself,
I suddenly lie against the naked breast of life, and her arms
round me are so gentle and so protective and my own
heartbeat is difficult to describe: so slow and so regular
and so soft, almost muffled, but so constant, as if it would
never stop. That is also my attitude to life, and I believe
that neither war nor any other senseless human atrocity
will ever be able to change it.[1]

Notice what Robert Ellsberg has called the "earthy and embodied" sense of the divine that saturates Hillesum's diaries. "For
Etty, everything—the physical and the spiritual without dis-
tinction—was related to her passionate openness to life, which
was ultimately openness to God."[2] Our bodies, the trees, the
earth—even the hard soil beneath the camps—pulses with the
whisper and protest of life itself, enfolding us "in her gentle and
regular heartbeat."

Etty was no naïve romantic. She felt the noose tightening, the
impending "cruelty and deprivation the likes of which I cannot
imagine in even my wildest fantasies." Yet there pulses throughout her diaries an enduring sense of grace and consolation: "I
don't feel [caught] in anybody's clutches; I feel safe in God's arms,
to put it rhetorically, and no matter whether I am sitting at this
beloved old desk now, or in a bare room in the Jewish district, or

perhaps in a labor camp under SS guards in a month's time—I shall always feel safe in God's arms. . . . [All] this is as nothing to the immeasurable expanse of my faith in God and my inner receptiveness."[3]

The key image may be the last: her determination to maintain an "inner receptiveness" that no amount of barbed wire or ideological fury could contain. Indeed, Etty's journals reflect an inner freedom and faith that seem to flow much more from sensual receptivity and wordless silence than from any explicit religious creed or ritual action. "Such words as 'god' and 'death' and 'suffering' and 'eternity' are best forgotten," she writes. "We have to become as simple and as wordless as the growing corn or the falling rain. We must just be."[4] Etty's sensual openness to God included her closest friendships and intimate sexual relationships. With lovers no less than friends, family, and children, we must learn to "just be," attentive and unconditionally present, whether in passing ecstasies, in evening laughter around the dinner table, or in long passages of dryness and mutual loneliness. So is the way of friendship with God, who shares our desire, our solitude, our companionship, our loneliness.

Two weeks before her internment at Westerbork, Etty speaks directly to God, confessing her growing realization that the perceived presence or absence of the divine in the world depends considerably on us, on our "safeguarding" God's hidden dynamism within creation.

Sunday morning prayer. "Dear God, these are anxious times. Tonight for the first time I lay in the dark with burning eyes as scene after scene of human suffering passed before me. I shall promise You one thing, God, just one very small thing: I shall never burden my today with cares about my tomorrow, although that takes some practice. Each day is sufficient unto itself. I shall try to help You, God, to stop my strength ebbing away, though I cannot vouch for it in advance. But one thing is becoming increasingly clear to me: that You cannot help us, that we must help You to help ourselves. And that is all we can manage these days and also all that really matters: that we safeguard that little piece of You, God, in ourselves. And perhaps in others as well. . . . You cannot help us, but we must help You and defend Your dwelling place inside us to the last."[5]

Like many other stories of courage and resistance during the Holocaust, what most defies rational explanation in Etty's story was her willingness to take suffering upon herself "in solidarity with those who suffer." This was not a masochistic embrace of suffering for its own sake, as Ellsberg notes, but rather a vocation "to redeem the suffering of humanity from within, by safeguarding 'that little piece of You, God, in ourselves.'"[6] *To redeem the suffering of humanity from within*: black or white, Jew or Christian, Hindu or Muslim, Buddhist or atheist—is this not what it means to live in solidarity with friends and strangers alike in the merciful womb of Love? For Christians, does this not describe the very life and person of Jesus Christ?

No matter how often I read the diaries of Etty Hillesum, when I turn the final pages I am overwhelmed with both wonder and sadness. So much vitality, so much erotic warmth and humane goodness, snuffed out by the fury of racist ideology, set into motion with a technocratic efficiency and scope beyond all imagining. Etty's last known writings were scribbled on a postcard thrown from the train that delivered her to Auschwitz. "We left the camp singing," she wrote.[7]

It is not for me, let alone any Christian, to claim the victory for love, and thus for God, by Etty Hillesum's witness. And yet an almost miraculous spirit endures and comes to life again in our remembering her. Here I want to linger a moment longer with the striking feminine imagery that Etty uses to express her sense of God's presence, "her arms round me" so close and protective that she can scarcely distinguish it from her own heartbeat.

Of course, Etty is not the first Jew to express the divine encompassing Presence in such vividly feminine terms. From the books of Proverbs and Wisdom to the wisdom sayings of Jesus and many of the earliest christological hymns of the New Testament, the feminine face of God haunts the Bible itself, even where she has largely been marginalized or banished from institutional Judaism and Western Christianity. She saturates Jewish kabbalism's mystical narrative of *zimzum* (Hebrew: "contraction"), in which God creates and nurtures the world not through sheer omnipotence or dominating power but rather more like a mother, freely and lovingly opening a space in God's very self for the emergence of the material cosmos and consummately for human freedom. Paradoxically, it is the emptiness or womb-like openness of God's expansive love that sustains the ripening fullness of a vibrantly unfolding creation. But what can such feminine imagery have to do with racist genocide or the collective horrors of human history?

In her breathtaking study, *The Female Face of God in Auschwitz*, Jewish theologian Melissa Raphael joins other contemporary feminist theologians in arguing that patriarchal or exclusively male images, discourses, and practices in synagogue and church have sanctioned a great deal of injustice, misogyny, and violence in society, in no small part by obscuring the female face of God: God's nurturing, indwelling presence known in the Hebrew Bible as Wisdom, Shekinah, Sophia, Spirit.[8] Patriarchal forces have veiled the feminine divine "to the point of disappearance," argues Raphael, perhaps nowhere more horrifically than in Auschwitz. Indeed, it is not altogether surprising, she suggests, that traditional Jewish theology, with its own patriarchal imagination, could not conceive how the all-powerful God of Moses and the prophets would have been so utterly powerless, so *impotent*, in the face of Auschwitz. In effect, traditional post-Holocaust approaches accuse God, as Raphael notes, for *not being patriarchal enough.*[9]

In truth, God was not wholly eclipsed in Auschwitz, Raphael suggests, but became incarnate in women who turned in compassion and bodily care toward one other, defying the most inhumane and desperate circumstances. With unsparing detail, Raphael unearths the largely ignored and forgotten stories of women in the camps who maintained the practices of Jewish prayer and ritual purification with whatever resources were available to them—not excluding their own bodily fluids where water was nowhere to be found.[10] Within the barbed-wire enclosure of the camps one woman's body bent in compassionate presence over another woman's or a child's body formed an encircling space where the divine presence could dwell, where God could be reconciled with humanity over against the patriarchal god of raw power, the false and idolatrous god of nation-states and National Socialism. Even (and especially) in Auschwitz, the most basic gestures of compassion constituted "a redemptive moment of human presence, a *staying there* against erasure"[11]—not only for women in the camps, but through them, for God.

Raphael tells the story of a woman who, torn from her husband and children by SS guards immediately after arriving at the camp, falls weeping on the frozen ground "with the flaming crematoria before her," when she suddenly feels two hands lay a garment around her shoulders. An old Frenchwoman had stepped forward, wrapping her in her own cloak, whispering "It will be over and done soon, it will be over."[12] Raphael recalls another now-iconic story of an old woman who is remembered "for holding in her arms a motherless 1-year-old child as she stood at the edge of the communal pit, about to be shot with the rest of her village by Nazi troops. The old woman sang to the child and tickled him under the chin until he laughed with joy. Then they were shot."[13]

Clearly, Raphael's case for the divine presence in Auschwitz does not hinge on numerical or otherwise logical analyses, as if hints and gestures of the good could cancel out the overwhelming weight of evil. Hers is not "a quantitative theology, contingent upon circumstance"; it is "a qualitative, ethical theology"[14] in which "the truly numinous spectacle was not the horror of the flaming chimneys but the *mysterium* of human love that is stronger than death, the *tremendum* of its judgment upon demonic hate, and the *fascinans* of its calling God back into a world which had cast her out."[15] Indeed, the sacramental imagination, as I would call it here, whether Jewish or Christian, is an impulse that "attaches very large meanings to very small signs."[16]

Let me risk a personal example much closer to home. Several years ago my wife and I adopted two children from Haiti. Immediately after our adopted son Henry was born, somewhere in the vast slum of Cite Soleil in Port-Au-Prince, his mother abandoned him in a latrine, believing she had been impregnated by an evil spirit. My wife and I were told this story of Henry's birth when we held him for the first time at the age of six months. We also learned that sometime after he was abandoned—we don't know whether it was minutes or hours—another woman from the area heard his cries and found the newborn struggling in the latrine, half-submerged in feces. The neighbor retrieved him, brought him back to his mother, and insisted that she take him to the orphanage. She did. Now the rationalist may hear this story and call it a happy accident of circumstance. I call it a miracle of grace, which brought Henry crying and fighting *for life* from one woman's womb into another's sheltering arms and, less than a year later, into my family's embrace.

Of course, for every story like ours there are ten thousand (and six million) more that defy theological meaning. Even ours is haunted by ambiguities. Can grace rise from the horror of an earthquake? Since the earthquake in Haiti of January 2010 I have often thought of Henry's birth mother and pray that God has freed her from whatever dark spirits, or abusive men, that may once have overshadowed her. Even still, when I contemplate this beautiful child who came to us, as it were, "in the fullness of time," from a chain of events and innumerable acts of other people's selflessness well beyond my capacity to understand, I cannot help but fall mute in wonder.

There is a beautiful teaching in the Jewish tradition called *tikkun olam*, a Hebrew phrase meaning "the reparation," the "making good," "the rescuing to make good of what is left of this smashed world."[17] The wellspring of *tikkun olam* is love received and love freely given, a fierce love that seeks justice and the flourishing of life for all God's children. Melissa Raphael in her study of Auschwitz gets it exactly right, I believe, when she concludes: the restoration or *tikkun* of the world "does not occupy a quantity of space and time; it is the theophanic possibility of a moment."[18] The fearful mystery of grace hinges precisely on the moment—the accumulated constellation of moments—in which we, and people we will never meet, say yes or no to love.

Collectively, what such moments reveal is a picture of God's power as manifest in the vulnerability and weakness of incarnate love. "Where the communal fabric of the world was being torn apart, human love was anticipating its renewal."[19] Where racist ideology sought to obliterate God as God-incarnate in the Jews, there were nevertheless women (and certainly there were men) who "made a sanctuary for the spark of the divine presence that saved it from being extinguished."[20] Here, I think, is a central Jewish insight, which Christian theology has too often obscured: God asks, God invites, God needs our participation in the indwelling drama of love. We encounter that same flash of incarnate presence in Etty Hillesum. The realization of God's own hope for the world, what Jesus calls the reign of God, hinges on our inner receptiveness, our fiat, our participation.

For Catholics, of course, and for Thomas Merton, not only Christ but also Mary stands as our model for the call to such participation. Thus from *Hagia Sophia: Through her wise answer, through her obedient understanding, through the sweet yielding consent of Sophia, God enters without publicity into the city of rapacious men.* But we must never forget that Mary's fiat, her deep attunement to the divine presence, had long been prepared in her, as it was for Jesus, by the people Israel, whose stories resound everywhere with the call of covenant relationship in history. Note how the word "presence" evokes a promise that is both spatial and temporal, and always (this is crucial) reciprocal: "I am here with you now, in this place, in this moment." Indeed not just *with* you, but *in* you, and you in me. *Be still and know that I am God / Be still and know that I am a human being / Be still and know that I am the Earth.*

The Earth indeed, from a sophianic perspective, is "the silent memory of the world that gives life and fruit to all." The Earth is she who "preserves everything in herself," she in whom "nothing perishes," not even the smallest and most forgotten of creatures.[21] Etty Hillesum frequently describes a sense of divine presence consoling her from within the silences of nature, as in "the jasmine [outside] and that piece of sky beyond my window."[22] Likewise, Melissa Raphael notes that when no person was capable of a kind word or compassionate touch amid the dehumanizing conditions of the camps, "inanimate natural objects could take on the functions of divine presence for women." Here she recounts Victor Frankl's story of a girl who told him as she lay dying that a bare chestnut tree "was the only friend she had in her loneliness and that she often talked to it." When Frankl asked the girl if the tree replied, she answered, "It said to me, 'I am here—I am here—I am life, eternal life.'" Raphael concludes: "If God has chosen Israel as God's vehicle of self-revelation then [such stories] must tell us something about the nature and posture of God's presence among us. It may seem little more than a tree stripped of its leaves by an untempered wind."[23]

We might think of other places today, mostly hidden and marginal places, where the protest of Life itself, of Earth, and a Mother-Love's rebellion against cruelty and arbitrary violence seeks to break through into a world increasingly engineered for war, for violence of an unspeakable kind against women and children, and for planetary destruction.

She rises from the threatened rainforests of the Amazon river basin, not least in their mournful lament for Sr. Dorothy Stang, murdered for her defense of the trees and indigenous culture. She speaks to us in the "Mothers of the Disappeared," who dance together in the Plaza de Mayo of Buenos Aires in silent remembrance of their missing sons and daughters, husbands and grandsons, sisters and granddaughters. She weeps and rises defiantly in the story of Somaly Mam and countless other Cambodian women and children sold into the horrors of sexual slavery, often by their own families. She hides in Hagar, the slave of Sarah and concubine of Abraham; in Mary Magdalene, witness to the crucifixion and resurrection but demoted and maligned in word and imagery down through the ages; and in all the hidden women of the Bible silenced or misread through the eyes of racism and patriarchy.[24] She echoes in the poetry of the late Maya Angelou, who speaks for all such women with fierce resilience and sass in her poem, "Still I Rise."[25]

She speaks in the resplendent sophianic icons of the Russian Orthodox tradition; in the pages of Georges Bernanos's mournful classic, *The Diary of a Country Priest*; in Sojourner Truth's still-electrifying "Ain't I a Woman"; and in the soulful storytelling of Bill Withers's "Grandma's Hands," live at Carnegie Hall in 1973. She sings in the musical artistry of Joni Mitchell, Billy Holiday, and Fannie Lou Hamer and from almost every page in Sue Monk Kidd's resplendent first novel, *The Secret Life of Bees*, where the image of the Black Madonna infuses hope into the life of a young white girl who has none. She cries out in the silent aftershocks of destroyed natural landscapes and in the faces of the global poor and victimized women and children of color.[26]

What binds these diverse narratives into one wondrous yet troubling mosaic is the affirmation of divine presence precisely, urgently, and most intensely in those persons and places written off by conventional wisdom as inhuman and God-forsaken. Indeed, where conventional wisdom about the real world registers no disconnect between our complacent worship of "God" and the systematic violation of women, children, and the planet itself, divine Wisdom cries out from the crossroads in protest, identifying herself especially with the little, the hidden, and the forgotten ones and with suffering earth, the Mother of all God's children. Neither blood nor political boundaries nor religion can contain the reach of God's loving presence. *She smiles, for though they have bound her, she cannot be a prisoner. Not that she is strong, or clever, but simply that she does not understand imprisonment.*

"She cannot be a prisoner," Merton writes, in a singular flash of hope. And yet, we know that she can, and is. Surely the unraveling of the world in our time is bound up with our ongoing violence against and willful sundering *of God*. As Jewish theologian Rita Gross puts it: "When the masculine and the feminine aspect of God have been reunited and the female half of humanity has been returned from exile, we will begin to have our *tikkun*. The world will be repaired."[27]

Who is Wisdom-Sophia? She is the divine Child in us who *refuses to be accommodated* to the world as dictated by "the people with watch chains,"[28] the men who make the trains run on time: trains loaded with priests and intellectuals steaming north into Siberia for the Gulag; trains bulging with Jews like so many cattle destined for the efficient slaughter; or, closer to home, trains loaded with metals stripped from the earth and now lumbering three shifts night and day into the sprawling GE plant outside Louisville, Kentucky, to feed our collective appetite for new refrigerators, automobiles, or the latest generation of drone aircraft now swarming the skies in the East, piloted by some kid sitting behind a computer screen in New Mexico. She is the Child in us who rejects the logic of the businessman, a bit drowsy after lunch, who says over his steak and martini: "Look kid, the sooner you grow up and learn to live in the real world the better."

She is the perplexity of a young Benjamin Braddock played by Dustin Hoffman in *The Graduate* when the husband of his ill-fated lover, Mrs. Robinson, corners him after graduation and says to him with utter conviction: "I've got one word for you, son: *plastics*." She is Sylvia in Peter Weir's brilliant film *The Truman Show*, who breaks onto the set to tell Truman, played with perfect, poignant innocence by Jim Carrey, that the world he lives in is a completely manufactured fiction. Hers is the face that haunts Truman and will not let him go. She is the one who reveals to Truman that he is not living, in fact, because he is not free. Sophia is that spirit of creativity and celebration *written into our very being*, yet feared and starved dead for oxygen by an institutional church that seems determined to rigidly choreograph and control every move in the dance. After all, as the logic of clericalism goes, the people in the pews "are not theologically trained."[29]

Hope in the key of Wisdom refuses to accommodate itself to the lock-tight logic of The Way Things Are as preached by the powers and principalities in society or church. This is the meaning of her innocence, and ours, when we open our imaginations to possibilities hidden yet manifest right before our eyes. *To risk opening our hearts to possibilities hidden yet manifest right before our eyes.* Here is the music that Merton heard in the long-neglected Wisdom tradition. In an atmosphere marked painfully by impasse and despair, Sophia sings words of unity and hope, of revelatory wonder and beauty. Above all, she summons us to freedom and full participation in the life story of God.

What does it mean, then, to live together with Wisdom? It is to live fully awake in the center of these contradictions of our times while refusing to be defined by them, to accommodate ourselves to them, like an essence fed into a computer. *For when I am home with her I can take my ease, for nothing is bitter in her company.*[30] This is what Merton, citing Julian of Norwich, calls the true "eschatological secret" of Christian hope and the very "heart of theology: not solving the contradiction, but remaining in the midst of it, in peace, knowing that it is fully solved, but that the solution is secret, and will never be guessed until it is revealed. . . . The wise heart lives in Christ."[31]

I believe that each of us comes from the creator trailing wisps of glory.

~ Maya Angelou

The Poetry of the earth is never dead.

~ John Keats

VIII

Breathe in the Air

*L*ate one afternoon several years ago in the midst of summer vacation at Sturgeon Bay in northern Michigan, my family packed a picnic and drove north with some close friends to arrive at the bay just before sunset. As we settled onto the beach and began to take in the moment, our adopted son Henry, then aged two-and-a-half, looked up from his food to catch the red-orange sun as it fell toward the water. He ambled down to the surf, and after a few minutes playing at the water's edge, he noticed the swirls of flaming light in the surf at his feet. Mesmerized, he turned his body and slowly raised his head, following the light as it danced across the luminous bay and out to the shimmering boundary where the crimson sun and purpling sky met the water. The rest of us sat on our beach blankets, mouths agape, watching the scene unfold. As the sun touched the water Henry raised both hands to the sky, one of them still clutching his sippy cup, and then—I'm not making this up—he began to chant and sing and sway from side to side. For what seemed like the next ten minutes, the child sang the sun into the water.

What in God's name was he singing? What compelled this child, who cannot stand still for thirty seconds, to remain fixed in that spot and sing with nonsensical abandon to the surf and sky? Anyone watching might have reasonably concluded it was nothing, an explosion of random neurons, a flurry of toddler gibberish. I'm not so sure. Perhaps he was singing the "forgotten mother tongue," the language of wonder and radical amazement, before he has a chance to grow up and forget. Maybe he was chanting his plain ecstasy before we, with our adult sophistication and sober "reality checks," have a chance to teach such music out of him!

In one of my favorite passages in all of his writings, Merton reflects on some children's drawings that were sent to the monastery from "somewhere in Milwaukee." After noting that the pictures are the "only real works of art I have seen in ten years," he continues, quite poignantly: "But it occurred to me that these wise children were drawing pictures of their own lives. They knew what was in their own depths. They were putting it all down on paper before they had a chance to grow up and forget."[1] What is Merton getting at here? What is it that lives and shines forth especially in children that we "grow up and forget," that we—academics, well-fed pundits, commonsense adults—so often fail to behold in the world, in ourselves, and especially in the stranger?

The great African American theologian and mystic Howard Thurman recalls a memory from his boyhood in Florida, walking on the beach at night "in the quiet stillness":

> when the murmur of the ocean is stilled and the tides
> move stealthily along the shore. I held my breath against

the night and watched the stars etch their brightness on the face of the darkened canopy of the heavens. I had the sense that all things, the sand, the sea, the stars, the night, and I were one lung through which all of life breathed. Not only was I aware of a vast rhythm enveloping all, but I was a part of it and it was a part of me.[2]

Do such moments teach us anything, *really*, about reality? In a word, are they trustworthy?

There are certain gifts that I cannot give to any person, impose on them, or ever steal away. One of these is the encounter with the mystery and wonder of life itself and with the greatest of all mysteries we name God. For Thurman, the experience of the sheer *gratuitousness* of life itself—unexpected, unearned, simply given—is the pulsing womb from which all other concerns ebb and flow, inclusive of social and political concerns. Here the individual stands "face to face with something which is so much more, and so much more inclusive, than all of his awareness of himself that for him, *in the moment*, there are no questions. Without asking, somehow he knows."

Knows what? The reality that we and all things in the universe are in fact "one lung" through which all of life breathes is not new, says Thurman. "The thing that is new is the *realization*. And this is of profound importance."[3] Indeed, this palpable sense of the unity of oneself and all things in God is so transforming that it leads the biblical psalmist and wisdom writers to surmise that there is in the human race an uncreated element, an eternal dimension. With Merton's help, we have called her Sophia, divine-human Wisdom, the Christ Child who hides and plays in all the people.

Herein lay the disarming paradox of religious experience. On the one hand, the realization of ourselves in God and in all things feels like something altogether new: it is "so much more, and so much more inclusive" than our default mode of consciousness, which divides the world into Subjects and Objects, Me and You, and, most ominously, Us and Them. On the other hand, when we come into an awareness of the whole—inclusive of God, not as object or separate being out there, but as "Thou" who seeks us as the Beloved, God as the One in whom we live and move and have our being—we come into possession, says Thurman, "of what [we have] known as being true all along."[4] It is like coming home to where we have never been before.

We reach feebly for language to utter such an insight: "sometimes it is called an encounter; sometimes, a confrontation; and sometimes, a sense of Presence."[5] Psychologists, religious philosophers, and skeptics alike have tried to classify, tame, and occasionally dismiss such experiences: they are "peak moments," possibly linked to the "ecology of imagination in childhood."[6] In truth, says Thurman, the encounter with God is "beyond or inclusive of" all such descriptive terms and attempts at rational, analytic control. The mind has to expand its palette through poetry, psalms, parables, and chant. The mark of God is written eternally on our forehead, says Thurman, citing the book of Job. God's own language of desire, what Rabbi Abraham Joshua Heschel calls the "forgotten mother tongue,"[7] is written eternally in our hearts.

Thurman calls the realization of God "the most daring and revolutionary concept" known to the human race: specifically, "that God is not only the creative mind and spirit at the core of the universe but that [God] . . . is love." Such a conclusion, he grants, cannot be arrived at "by mere or sheer rational processes. This is the great disclosure: that there is at the heart of life a Heart."[8] Nowhere are Thurman's writings more powerful or moving than where he writes of Jesus of Nazareth as the lens for this great disclosure of the Heart: Jesus, who had "what seems to me to have been a fundamental and searching—almost devastating—experience of God."[9]

> To Jesus, God breathed through all that is. The sparrow overcome by sudden death in its evening flight; the lily blossoming on the rocky hillside; the grass of the field and the garden path . . . ; the madman in chains or wandering among the barren rocks in the wastelands; the little baby in his mother's arms; the strutting arrogance of the Roman Legion; the brazen queries of the craven tax collector; the children at play or the old men quibbling in the market place; the august Sanhedrin fighting for its life amidst the impudences of Empire; the fear-voiced utterance of the prophets who remembered—to Jesus, God breathed through all that is.[10]

Repeatedly, Thurman draws our attention to how Jesus prayed, how often Jesus prayed, how Jesus' whole life *was* a continuous prayer. And repeatedly, he counsels us to do as Jesus did, to "wait in the quietness for some centering moment that will redefine, reshape, and refocus our lives."[11]

> The time most precious for him was at close of day. This was the time for the long breath, when all the fragments

left by the commonplace, when all the little hurts and the big aches could be absorbed, and the mind could be freed of the immediate demand, when voices that had been quieted by the long day's work could once more be heard, where there could be the deep sharing of the innermost secrets and the laying bare of the heart and mind. Yes, the time most precious for him was at close of day.[12]

The passage shares not a little with the closing scene of *Hagia Sophia*, where "the homeless God" lay down "under the sweet stars of the world" and entrusts himself to sleep.

Again, there are certain gifts that I cannot give to, impose on, or take away from any person. But I qualify: How often God can and does give such gifts through us, through our embodied presence, and through the communities of family, work, and faith to which we belong. My son Henry's reverie before the sunset was not mine to give. And yet our bringing him to that place of beauty, our sharing it with him, opened up a circle in time and space for the ordinary miracle that unfolded and so unexpectedly gifted us. Indeed, the gift that the Christian tradition calls "grace" plays and dances through our lives in so many spontaneous and unpredictable ways: in our awe before the beauty of nature; in kind gestures passed between a parent and child, between friends, or between colleagues at work; in "the long breath" and "deep sharing" between spouses or lovers at the close of the day. But torn from a sense of wonder, torn from the art of silence and stillness, torn from the discipline of exposure and surrender to the One who breathes through all that is, what hope for reconciling our fragmented selves, much less for building friendship and peace with strange others?

Why is the discipline of solitude and prayer crucial to the work for peace in the human community and reconciliation with the earth? Because, like a single lung, God breathes in and through all things. We lose touch with this fundamental insight to our great peril. Much like Merton, Heschel, and King, at the end of the day Thurman seems to ask: *Whose are we?* In whom do we place our ultimate trust? The source of life is God, who saturates all things in a sea of reverence. Can we see it? And can we afford "while the world around is so sick and weary and desperate" to bind our lives to such a contemplative foundation? Can we afford not to? "Do not shrink from moving confidently out into the choppy seas. Wade in the water, because God is troubling the water."[13]

"The confidence of the Christian," Merton writes, "is always a confidence in spite of darkness and risk, in the presence of peril, with every evidence of possible disaster."[14] Indeed, for all the mystics and prophets the spiritual life is not an escape from reality but a kind of wading into the deep of reality's troubled waters. The thing is: we do not plunge in alone. Jesus goes before us in the way of freedom and grace. The great disclosure who is Jesus teaches us how to live prayerfully from the Heart of God, which means not only to see and speak the truth but to see with eyes of mercy and love. To see and speak with love, of course, is a paschal option. It hurts. It takes time. It refuses blanket condemnations. It takes the time to linger not only in shadowlands and prison cells but also in courtyards where children play, in boats where fishermen work their nets, at weddings, on rocky hillsides, along garden paths, and in the foaming shoreline of the

Sea of Galilee—or Lake Michigan, for that matter! The cross, after all, for each of us in different ways, will come soon enough.[15]

There are gifts we cannot give to, impose on, or steal away from anybody. What we can do is *live*, like Jesus, and be present to each other and to the earth, and thus open circles in space and time for the gifts of God to break through. White and black, brown and red, Catholic and Protestant, Christian and Jew, Hindu and Muslim—we can wait together in the quietness "for some centering moment that will redefine, reshape, and refocus our lives."

Let me share one last story of sunset, a precious time of day anywhere on earth. Abraham Joshua Heschel's biographer recalls a poignant incident when the young Jewish student, having just arrived in Berlin to study at the university in 1927, was walking through its "magnificent streets" when he noticed that the sun had gone down, and suddenly realized that he had forgotten to pray. "I had forgotten God—I had forgotten Sinai—I had forgotten that sunset is my business—that my task is to 'restore the world to the kingship of the Lord.'"[16]

Twenty-five years later, having narrowly escaped the catastrophe engulfing the Jews of Europe, including the murder of his mother and three sisters, Heschel lamented still more our seeming imprisonment in the narrow confines of our own minds and the terrible costs to our humanity of being turned in upon the self: "We are rarely aware of the tangent of the beyond at the whirling wheel of experience. . . . What is extraordinary appears to us as habit, the dawn a daily routine of nature. But time and again we awake. In the midst of walking in the never-ending procession of days and nights, we are suddenly filled with a solemn terror, with a feeling of our wisdom being inferior to dust. We cannot endure the heartbreaking splendor of sunsets."[17]

The twilight at sunset is a boundary condition, a liminal space, a fluid borderland where we delight for a while in the haunting indeterminacies of the light in-between. The life of the God-haunted, it seems to me, is much like the twilight, a strange dwelling place of in-betweens where humanity and divinity, life and death, joy and sorrow, ecstasy and despair, *commingle*, and every moment is pregnant with expectation. The great difficulty for the religious person is to live with trust, even confidence, in the beautiful but perilous twilight spaces of our pilgrimage in history. The future is not a homogenous and empty time for the believer. "Do not be afraid," the Scriptures counsel repeatedly. Have faith. God is truly with us, and God comes passionately toward us from the future.

IX

To Say Something Worthy
of God

The whole of this book has circled around the question of God, and thus, the struggle for faith, hope, and love, in unsettling times. What reasons can we give for our hope in a God who loves and bears with us patiently, a God of the Beatitudes who commands us to study war no more, a God of resurrection who scatters seeds of life even in fresh fields of death? What justifications can we offer for *God's faith in us* to be sowers of justice and peace in the world? Is our addiction to violence a symptom of despair in God's capacity for mercy, or our own? Jesus' command to love our enemies, after all, presumes our graced capacity to do so. Is Christ's trust in us misplaced? So much depends on our image of God! So much depends on our idea of humanity! "If love or nonviolence be not the law of our being," confesses Mahatma Gandhi, "the whole of my argument falls to pieces."[1]

97

As Merton relentlessly reminded his contemporaries, the social ills facing our generation are not abstract issues "out there" for the Christian, nor can they be deflected as problems of "history." We are all guilty bystanders, standing under judgment and responsibility to repair the world. But under *whose* judgment do we stand: a distant, all-powerful, "solid marble God"[2] who settles himself grimly in our frozen hearts, or a God whose patient tenderness and deference to human freedom (picture the father in Jesus' parable of the Prodigal Son) exposes our sins in the light of Love and Mercy? In the former case, violence and retribution too easily mask as religious commandments by which we become the self-justifying vehicles of "divine justice." In the latter, we move through the world, as the great Maya Angelou put it, "trailing wisps of glory,"[3] empowered by grace to be bearers of hospitality and truth telling, peace and reconciliation, even unto death. So much depends on our image of God. So much depends on our idea of humanity.

If Merton would be our guide, the naming of God is not about circumscribing God with this or that political badge or theological button and then trying to get as many people as you can by threat or persuasion to pin your God-badge on their chest. The naming of God involves the sensitive discernment of who God is in relationship to who we are through long meditation on the images and poetical symbols that shine through quietly, or break through dangerously, from the revelatory firmament of the Bible. To name is not primarily to *identify*; to name is to reveal (and shape) a person's deepest *identity*. To know someone's name, in the biblical tradition, is to know something fundamental about them. Names in the Bible convey meaning. They unveil. They unmask.[4]

In Merton's life we behold the unveiling of Sophia, who is God herself and God's freedom for love coming alive in all creation. As the power of God's mercy, Merton dares to suggest, she makes possible in us *miracles greater even than the creation*: the work of patient listening and understanding, truth telling, joy making, and peace. In Wisdom's house there is room for all. In *my* house, teeming with four kids, she sows forbearance, laughter, dancing around the dinner table to the music of Stevie Wonder, and unexpected joy, when all reserves seem to have run dry.

Notwithstanding its highly philosophical and distinctive cultural content, the Russian Sophia tradition begins and ends in the ecstasy of love, of being loved gratuitously by God, spilling over into an embodied sense of unity with all things. Yet rising from this mysticism of grace and of "being at home" in the physical universe, the Wisdom tradition gives voice at once to a deep sense of exile, historical urgency and danger, a prophetic cry "from the crossroads" to hear and respond to God's revelatory word in history. As we have seen, Merton's awakening to Sophia in the last decade of his life was cut from much the same cloth as Bulgakov's had been in the wake of the horrors of the Russian Revolution and two world wars: namely, the cloth of protest.

In Merton's case, the embrace of Wisdom-Sophia marked a protest against the "flight from woman" wounding his own past, and perhaps even crippling the prospects for renewal in the Catholic Church. Clearly it marked a deeper integration of the feminine in himself and a fuller acceptance of his own capacity to love and allow himself to be loved in return. But no less prescient was his protest against the deadly "seriousness" of American power and its Promethean grasping for life that plays out tragically, in fact, as an addiction to death. Under a reigning collective consciousness bent on war and its endless preparation, the sophianic Child—and real children everywhere—lay forgotten, dead, buried. Christian "eschatology" in such an atmosphere becomes little more than "the last gasp of exhausted possibilities,"[5] our secret desire to get it all over with.

As I write these lines, the world's attention has been fixed on the plight of hundreds of teenage girls in northern Nigeria, kidnapped at gunpoint from their boarding school by the Islamist extremist group Boko Haram—a name that translates figuratively as "Western education is sin." One shudders to imagine the fate of these girls, sadly symbolic of the cultural and literal bodily enslavement suffered by far too many women and girls across the world today. Of course, any honest appraisal of these events must also take into account the history of Western (and Christian) imperialism in Nigeria. Also symbolic of the latent power of young women in oppressive contexts, Pakistani teenager Malala Yousafzai was recently honored by the United Nations on her sixteenth birthday. Shot in the head by the Taliban for her advocacy of girls' education, "She was targeted," UN Secretary General Ban Ki-moon said, "just because of her determination to go to school. The extremists showed what they fear most—a girl with a book."[6] Is it wrong-headed, naïve, or culturally imperialist of me to wonder: What image/idol of "God," what distorted vision of humanity, lurks beneath such unspeakable crimes against human dignity?[7] Malala Yousafzai gives us, in biblical terms, another glimpse of the *anawim*, the still, small voice of Sophia breaking through in our time.

Much closer to home, in the culturally "liberated" and "Christian" United States, reputable data suggests that at least one in five women are victims of sexual assault, typically perpetrated by boyfriends, husbands, or acquaintances, while educators and mental health professionals struggle to respond to what many describe as a "rape culture" on college campuses. A recent campus shooting in California exposes what one analyst has described—accurately, I fear—as "a cultural undercurrent of a seething-to-subtle hatred of women, especially among an emerging cohort of apparently self-entitled, angry and occasionally violent young men."[8] The alienation of young boys and girls alike is stoked by a confusing swirl of contradictory messages around sexuality, gender, and power inside a subterranean internet porn and video gaming culture, all fueled by a consumerist and media-driven society. Ten or twenty years from now what will be the impact on human lives and relationships of a widespread addiction, especially among boys, to images of sexualized violence? And obviously, tragically, the church is no safe haven from personal and institutionalized sin, or from predatory cultural forces that impact everybody. The revelation of widespread sexual abuse of children in the Roman Catholic Church and systematic denial and obfuscation by bishops around the world continues to this day.[9]

Elementally, it seems the deepest wounds in us are not strictly or necessarily about gender or sex or power as such but about the grotesque malformation of freedom in us, male and female alike, that would seek to *blot out the light* in others or fail to protect and nurture the divinity in ourselves or another creature. To speak biblically, the evil spirit who *fears, hates, and envies the light* finds a too-docile home in us! Too easily we "lay our glory by"[10] and by our choices, both personal and institutional, we diminish the glory of others.

And what can we say of the suffering Earth, the home and mother of all? Rather than survey the litany of climate scientists shouting from the rooftops for the rest of us to please wake up, perhaps it is enough to cite just one, Bill McKibben, whose soulful lament, *The End of Nature*, evokes in me the unsettling image of a train hurtling slow-motion like toward a bridge that is *no longer there*, its passengers complacently oblivious to their terrible fate.[11] Such images, if they do not paralyze us, give rise to thought: what words of hope can we offer the next generation?

In his classic study, *The Prophetic Imagination*, biblical scholar Walter Brueggemann identifies one of the crucial tasks of prophetic imagination as "the *offering of symbols* that are adequate to contradict a situation of hopelessness in which newness is unthinkable." This voicing of hope "cannot be done by inventing new symbols," however, "for that is wishful thinking. Rather it means to move back into the deepest memories of community and activate those very symbols that have always been the basis for contradicting the regnant consciousness."[12] It is not unreasonable, I think, from a truly global and planetary perspective, to describe our present historical moment as approximating a "situation of hopelessness in which newness is unthinkable." More and more life everywhere seems threatened and colonized by a "regnant consciousness" that makes wholeness, justice, and peace seem not merely difficult but well-nigh impossible. Yet it is precisely from within this dark breach, as Brueggemann suggests, in the silences between lamentation and despair, the prophet seeks to retrieve and activate the community's deepest symbols of memory, resistance, and hope. To say it another way, the prophet and poet "must speak for a silent God."[13]

Maybe it is too much to expect the Christian community *en masse* to go into the terrible breach where the prophets have gone. But if Brueggemann's insight may be applied to our pastors and religious leaders, then to think prophetically in our times must be *to pray* theologically for a word of hope where things look hopeless, for a renewed sense of presence where God feels absent, for a memory of healing and liberation where relationships seem broken or coercive beyond repair. This remembering and naming of our deepest identity in God is, I believe, what Merton discovered in the music of the Wisdom tradition. In that pregnant space between divine invitation and creation's response, something new and wordlessly ancient waits to be born into the world, something beautiful, in the very flesh and spirit of our lives: *Sophia*. But can we believe it? As Brueggemann says of Jesus and the prophets, as Merton says of Pasternak, maybe it is the poet, after all, who will "help us get back to ourselves before it is too late."[14]

But why not also the theologian? Consider again Merton's earliest notes on the Russian Sophia tradition: "Bulgakov and Berdyaev are writers of great, great attention. . . . They have dared to accept the challenge of the sapiential books, the challenge of the image of Proverbs where Wisdom is 'playing in the world' before the face of the Creator."[15] What stands out so clearly in Merton's engagement with the Russian writers is his admiration for their theological creativity, their willingness to make mistakes "in order to say something great and worthy of God." "One wonders," he muses, "if our theological cautiousness is not after all the sign of a fatal coldness of heart, an awful sterility born of fear, or of despair."[16] Indeed, one wonders! But the Sophia tradition also dares to say something great and worthy of humanity. In a word, as Merton wondered at Fourth and Walnut, how do you tell people that they are walking around shining like the sun? He found his answer in the remembrance of Proverb, Wisdom, Sophia.

What graces might come to the world if we remembered God not only as Person, as in Jesus Christ, but as a Woman, calling out at the crossroads urging all the peoples of the world to *see* and relate to one another as members of one diverse but radically interdependent family? As a Mother, bent over her children in fierce protection, or crowning them with purpose and strength for the difficult journey ahead?[17] As a Child, playing joyfully in the mountains, deserts, and watercourses of creation? As a Lover, not abstract and fleshless, but as one who loves us precisely in and through our bodies and who, despite our failings, still holds us in mercy and calls forth something strong and beautiful in us, something that we have "long ago ceased to be"?[18] As Sister, Companion, Friend?

What healing might rise in our own small circle of the world if we—male and female alike—embodied Sophia more intentionally and fiercely in our various ways, in our families, institutions, and worldly occupations? What would it *feel like* to think and pray with a God who is not fixed like a Great Marble Statue in the elite or far-away spaces where power is exercised but who enters without reserve into the stream of our humble tasks, decisions, and everyday commitments? Such a God would ignite our hope, which is the capacity to breathe and to imagine again.

To be clear, as a father myself, as the son of a loving father, the paternal face of God evokes beautifully for me Christianity's sublime teachings about love, both human and divine. For many men, women, and children, "Father" has long been and will forever be an empowering divine image, a sustaining metaphor of divine presence, constancy, and loving care (picture the father in Rembrandt's incomparable *The Return of the Prodigal Son*). Yet for many whose experience of "father" is traumatic, domineering, or cold, the image does not evoke or make room enough for love. For many, the line between paternal presence and patriarchal power is much too thin. We must remember that God is also Mother, Spirit, and Shekhinah, lest we deny our maternal and feminine experiences of grace, tighten the noose around divine and human wholeness, and foreclose the imaginative flexibility of the Bible itself, not to mention the great intellectual and mystical tradition of the church. With Christians from East to West for nearly two millennia, my own prayer life has been enormously enlarged and enriched by the biblical image and memory of God as Sophia, as Holy Wisdom. I hope and trust the same will be true for my children. How, then, to realize her presence more palpably in the practices that shape our world and our church?[19]

Without question, all gender-bound metaphors for the divine are inadequate, since God is not an object of knowledge. It is also

significant that Merton uses gendered metaphors interchange-
ably in *Hagia Sophia* to suggest a God beyond traditional gender
binaries.[20] Yet we should not be too quick to move "beyond"
feminine images and names of God prior to having lingered with
them for a very long while, allowing depths of memory, thought,
and feeling to rise to the surface. By "we," I mean first of all the
Roman Catholic and Christian communities from East to West
who share the same Scriptures. But the point radiates outward
today, and urgently, to include Jews and Muslims and any other
communities whose religious imaginations—and therefore families, communities, societies—also call for the healing of patriarchal deformations. It is a delicate thought experiment, to be
sure, but by no means a gratuitous one in an era such as ours, in
which oppressed women, men, and children "have their history
inscribed on their bodies."[21]

The realization of Jesus and Jesus *crucified* as Wisdom incarnate reinforces the point powerfully. For Christ is crucified
still in the bodies of the hungry, the lonely, the tortured, the lost,
the exterminated. The crucifixion of Jesus unveils the night face
of Sophia—Sophia bound up in "pain, trouble, pestilence." The
name Sophia reinforces what Christian theology claims for all,
both in our joys and in our sorrows: that, in and through Christ
Jesus, God has approached and assumed all humanity, integrally,
bodily, into the very life of God, not merely a segment of humanity or an aspect of the human condition. The alternative, "that
womanhood is not included in what has been assumed,"[22] or
the poor, the criminal, the immigrant, the non-Christian, the
homosexual, and so on, is theologically absurd. The love of God

in Christ and through the Spirit knows no bounds (Gal 3:28; Rom 8:38-39).

Again and again in the gospels we see Jesus challenging the conventional wisdom of his society and reordering all relationships under the demanding light of God's care for all, the "innocent" and "guilty" alike. Justice in the parables of Jesus is measured not by retribution or *quid pro quo* but by the restoration of right relationships in communion with God, earth, one another. To Jesus, God breathes "like a single lung" through all that is. Jesus responds to all things in the light of God's scandalously inclusive love. To live "in Christ" is to strain every muscle to do and *to be* likewise. Father or Mother, Sister or Brother, in our acts of compassion we share in the very life of God. Then, there is no separation. We become God's presence in the world. Blessed are the peacemakers, of every creed, for they shall be called daughters and sons of God.

Certainly it is fair to ask whether Merton and his sophiological forebears, in their visions and dreams of Sophia, were not *merely* dreaming. How is the mind to make sense of it? On the other hand, might these poets, prophets, and philosophers of Wisdom be giving voice to our own deepest intuition that something essential, beautiful, and true has been lost in the life story of God? *Sophia, the feminine child, is playing in the world, obvious and unseen, playing at all times before the Creator.* Of course, to answer in the affirmative is not to claim a rational proof or "explanation." As in all prayerful discernment, one has to test everything received in light of everything given anew to our minds, senses, and the eyes of our hearts. But let us also remember, as Sandra Schneiders reminds us, that just as images of the self and world can be healed, "so can the God-image. It cannot be healed, however, by rational intervention alone."[23]

In the midst of all such questions—and at once breaking free of them—Merton gives voice to a disarming but wondrous hope: *She smiles, for though she is bound, she cannot be a prisoner.*[24] And that hope, nourished by sustained meditation and discernment, may come to breathe in us like unto a prayer. Like a star breaking into view from the revelatory firmament of the Bible, may Wisdom arise in our consciousness like the remembrance of the forgotten mother tongue, awakening us from nightmarish dreams of separateness and drawing us back into the realization of our radical kinship in God and unity of love. We do not have to go so far to catch echoes of her invitation, "for it beats in our very blood, whether we want it to or not."[25]

I conclude with my thanks to the reader and the many generous people who have shared with me their insights and wisdom in conversations rising from this material. The widening circle of friendship that I have known in the Merton community near and far, the committed lives of peacemaking and humane scholarship, is one of the great blessings of my life. Whether new to Merton's writings or long familiar, in the decades since his death not a few have wondered what particular magic continues to attract people of every generation and such wildly diverse backgrounds to Merton. The answer, I think, is as close as our own humanity. "Like each of us," writes Susan McCaslin, "Merton was flawed." But what matters "is the constant evolution of both his life and his work—the always surging, expanding presence. The way he makes a gift of his own fragility gives us hope that each of us, with our own finitudes, flaws and failures, may also touch holy ground. He's not removed from us, but a brother."[26]

One hundred years after his birth, and almost fifty years since his death, Merton still walks beside us as a brother. For the gift of his life and witness, I give thanks. Thomas Merton "was a God-oriented man leading like-minded people on the way of the Gospel." He was a friend of God.

Acknowledgments

*I*n July 1968, not long after the assassinations of Martin Luther King Jr. and Robert F. Kennedy, and reflecting on the tides of change in the Roman Catholic Church in the wake of Vatican II, Merton wrote to his friend and fellow monk Jean Leclercq: "The vocation of the monk in the world is not survival but prophecy. We are all too busy saving our skins." Five months later in Bangkok, Thailand, just hours before his death, Merton voiced a similar sentiment, quoting from His Holiness the Dalai Lama: "From now on, everybody stands on his own feet. . . . The time for relying on structures has disappeared."

The dichotomy suggested in these two statements is a tempting but ultimately, I think, false one. As bears out powerfully in Merton's own life and spirituality, everything depends on the peaceful attunement of opposite tensions. Prophecy, especially today, needs the survival of institutions if it is to have real social impact. The power of Merton's prophetic voice depended in no small part on his embeddedness in and commitment to the monastic, ecclesial, literary, and politically engaged communities of which he was but one integral part. At the end of the day nobody "stands on his own feet," not even Thomas Merton.

In the development of these conferences I am indebted to many wonderful people, institutions, communities, "structures." First, I wish to thank the people who have hosted me so graciously and offered invaluable feedback in the following places: Wisdom House Retreat Center (Lichtfield, CT); the Institute for Religion and Science (Chestnut Hill College, PA); Northeast Guild for Spiritual Formation (Bass Harbor, ME); Jesuit Spiritual Center (Milford, OH); Transfiguration Spirituality Center (Cincinnati, OH); and Saint Monica–Saint George Parish Newman Center (Cincinnati, OH). Especially to Ann Boltz at Saint Monica–Saint George, thank you for seeing and affirming in me gifts that I didn't know I had. Likewise, the higher learning communities of Regis University in Denver and the University of Notre Dame have been generous homes for me and my family at pivotal stages in my formation as a Catholic teacher and theologian.

Since my first book on Merton was published I've been gifted beyond words by the friendship of artists deeply attuned to the Spirit whose lives and work give expression in distinct ways to the unveiling of Sophia in our times: iconographer William Hart McNichols (fatherbill.org); South African writer Rosemary Kearney (themagdalenetestament.com); Canadian poet Susan McCaslin (members.shaw.ca/smccaslin); and Cincinnati painters Holly Schapker (hollyschapker.com) and Katherine Colborn (katherinecolborn.com). I've also been sustained immeasurably by my students and colleagues at Xavier University and the worldwide community of support and friendship I've come to know through the International Thomas Merton Society.

From my childhood to the present day, Catholic women religious have shown me what friendship with God and fidelity to the church looks like, in their lives of contemplation, prayerful discernment, and creative action. Special thanks to my beloved Aunt Mary, a.k.a. Sister Chris Doherty, OSF, a.k.a. "The Cloth"; Sister Kathleen Duffy, SSJ; and Sister Anita Baird, DHM, for her witness to the beauty, wonder, and tenacity of African American Catholic spirituality. The way is not easy, but God is faithful, and that indeed is our hope.

Once again to Liturgical Press: how can I adequately thank you for giving me and so many others a venue for our scholarship in service of the people of God? Your encouragement and tireless attention to the "small stuff" add up to a tremendous gift to society, the academy, and the church at every level.

And finally to my wife Lauri, in whose eyes I still see "the doorway to a thousand churches." From my heart I thank you for all the adventures we've shared together and for those yet to come. *Intrans in domum meam, conquiescam cum illa: non enim habet amaritudinem conversatio illius, sed laetitiam et gaudium.*

* * *

Page 12: Photograph of Thomas Merton. Copyright the Merton Legacy Trust and the Thomas Merton Center at Bellarmine University. Used with permission.

Front cover and pages xiv, 40, 50, and 96: Drawings by Thomas Merton. Copyright the Merton Legacy Trust and the Thomas Merton Center at Bellarmine University. Used with permission.

Page 70: Photograph of Etty Hillesum. Collection Jewish Historical
    Museum, Amsterdam.
Back cover photo: © The Estate of Ralph Eugene Meatyard, courtesy
    Fraenkel Gallery, San Francisco.

The following permission was in process at time of publication: Excerpts
    from *Emblems of a Season of Fury* (New York: New Directions, 1963)
    and *The Way of Chuang Tzu* (New York: New Directions, 1965).

Abbreviations

AJ	Thomas Merton. *The Asian Journal of Thomas Merton.* Edited by Naomi Burton Stone, Patrick Hart, and James Laughlin. New York: New Directions, 1973.
CGB	Thomas Merton. *Conjectures of a Guilty Bystander.* New York: Doubleday, 1966.
CT	Thomas Merton. *The Courage for Truth: The Letters of Thomas Merton to Writers.* Edited by Christine M. Bochen. New York: Farrar, Straus and Giroux, 1993.
DQ	Thomas Merton. *Disputed Questions.* New York: Harcourt Brace, 1960.
DWL	Thomas Merton. *Dancing in the Water of Life: Seeking Peace in the Hermitage.* Edited by Robert E. Daggy. San Francisco: HarperSanFrancisco, 1997.
ESF	Thomas Merton. *Emblems of a Season of Fury.* New York: New Directions, 1963.
GNV	*Gandhi on Non-Violence: Selected Texts from Mohandas K. Gandhi's Non-Violence in Peace and War.* Edited by Thomas Merton. New York: New Directions, 1965.

HGL   Thomas Merton. *The Hidden Ground of Love: The Letters of Thomas Merton on Religious Experience and Social Concerns.* Edited by William H. Shannon. New York: Farrar, Straus and Giroux, 1985.

HTEW   Howard Thurman. *Howard Thurman: Essential Writings.* Selected with an introduction by Luther E. Smith. Maryknoll, NY: Orbis, 2006.

ICM   Thomas Merton. *An Introduction to Christian Mysticism: Initiation into the Monastic Tradition 3.* Edited by Patrick F. O'Connell. Kalamazoo, MI: Cistercian Publications, 2008.

LTL   Thomas Merton. *Learning to Love: Exploring Solitude and Freedom.* Edited by Christine M. Bochen. San Francisco: HarperSanFrancisco, 1997.

MHPH   *Merton and Hesychasm: Prayer of the Heart.* Edited by Bernadette Dieker and Jonathan Montaldo. Louisville, KY: Fons Vitae, 2003.

NSC   Thomas Merton. *New Seeds of Contemplation.* New York: New Directions, 1961.

RU   Thomas Merton. *Raids on the Unspeakable.* New York: New Directions, 1966.

SFS   Thomas Merton. *A Search for Solitude: Pursuing the Monk's Life.* Edited by Lawrence S. Cunningham. San Francisco: HarperSanFrancisco, 1996.

SJ   Thomas Merton. *The Sign of Jonas.* New York: Octagon, 1983; original 1953.

SSM   Thomas Merton. *The Seven Storey Mountain.* New York: Harcourt Brace Jovanovich, 1948.

TTW   Thomas Merton. *Turning Toward the World: The Pivotal Years.* Edited by Victor A. Kramer. San Francisco: HarperSanFrancisco, 1997.

WF   Thomas Merton. *Witness to Freedom: The Letters of Thomas Merton in Times of Crisis.* Edited by William H. Shannon. New York: Harcourt Brace, 1995.

ZBA   Thomas Merton. *Zen and the Birds of Appetite.* New York: New Directions, 1968.

Notes

Introduction—pages ix–xii

1. Christopher Pramuk, *Sophia: The Hidden Christ of Thomas Merton* (Collegeville, MN: Liturgical Press / Michael Glazier, 2009).

2. Thomas Merton, *Hagia Sophia*, in *Emblems of a Season of Fury* (New York: New Directions, 1963), 61, 63; hereafter ESF.

3. Thomas Merton, *Conjectures of a Guilty Bystander* (New York: Doubleday, 1966), 132; hereafter CGB.

4. ESF, 62, 64.

5. Timothy Fry, "Preface," in *The Rule of St. Benedict in English*, ed. Timothy Fry (Collegeville, MN: Liturgical Press, 1982), 13.

I—pages 1–11

1. Thomas Merton, *The Sign of Jonas* (New York: Octagon, 1983), 349; hereafter SJ.

2. SJ, 349.

3. ESF, 61.

4. ESF, 63.

5. Andrew Greeley, "The Apologetics of Beauty," *America* 183, no. 7 (2000): 8–12.

6. Merton to Abdul Aziz, *The Hidden Ground of Love: The Letters of Thomas Merton on Religious Experience and Social Concerns*, ed. William H. Shannon (New York: Farrar, Straus and Giroux, 1985), 46; hereafter HGL.

7. Thomas Merton, *A Search for Solitude: Pursuing the Monk's Life*, ed. Lawrence S. Cunningham (San Francisco: HarperSanFrancisco, 1996), 197; hereafter SFS.

8. For the following biographical overview I am indebted to Christine Bochen, "Awakening the Heart," in *Thomas Merton: Essential Writings* (Maryknoll, NY: Orbis, 2000), 21–49; and Jonathan Montaldo, "Thomas Merton's Dialogues with Silence," in *Thomas Merton, Dialogues with Silence: Prayers and Drawings*, ed. Jonathan Montaldo (New York: HarperSan-Francisco, 2001), ix–xviii.

9. Thomas Merton, *The Seven Storey Mountain* (New York: Harcourt Brace Jovanovich, 1948), 13–16; hereafter SSM.

10. Susan McCaslin, "Thomas Merton, Citizen of the World," in *We Are Already One: Thomas Merton's Message of Hope*, ed. Gray Henry and Jonathan Montaldo (Louisville: Fons Vitae, 2015), 29–33, at 31.

11. SSM, 404.

12. SSM, 215.

13. SSM, 108.

14. SSM, 109. As Christine Bochen observes, "Merton discovered Christ, became a Christian, and found out what it meant to be a Christian—in that order" ("Awakening the Heart," 30).

15. SSM, 111.

16. Thomas Merton, *The Asian Journal of Thomas Merton*, ed. Naomi Burton Stone, Patrick Hart, and James Laughlin (New York: New Directions, 1973), 313; hereafter AJ.

17. Bochen, "Awakening the Heart," 48.

II—pages 13–25

1. CGB, 177. For a thorough exposition of Merton's nature writings, see Thomas Merton, *When the Trees Say Nothing: Writings on Nature*, ed. Kathleen Deignan (Notre Dame, IN: Sorin, 2003); and Monica Weis, *The Environmental Vision of Thomas Merton* (Lexington: University of Kentucky, 2011).

2. The term "communion" for Merton connotes a realization of "unity-in-difference" where unity does not imply uniformity: "We are all one silence and a diversity of voices." Merton frequently contrasts authentic "community" with the "collective" or "mass society." In the collective, un-yielding conformity is expected and difference regarded as a threat. In authentic community, difference is honored and the practices of solitude and contemplation protect the transcendent dignity of the person and individual conscience. See especially Thomas Merton, "Rain and the Rhinoceros," in *Raids on the Unspeakable* (New York: New Directions, 1966), 9–25; hereafter RU.

3. SFS, 214–15.

4. William Harmless, *Desert Christians: An Introduction to the Literature of Early Monasticism* (New York: Oxford University Press, 2004), 392.

5. CGB, 156–57.

6. "Innocence" and "paradise" are prominent themes in the Merton-Suzuki dialogue. See Thomas Merton, *Zen and the Birds of Appetite* (New York: New Directions, 1968), 99–141; hereafter ZBA. By "innocence" Merton does not suggest a regression to the freshness of childhood in a naïve or narcissistic sense, still less a denial of sin. Negatively, innocence means the refusal to accommodate oneself to or passively accept "the way things are" in mass society; positively, it speaks to "a new birth, the divine birth in us" that grounds our freedom and creativity in history as co-creators before God. See "Message to Poets," in RU, 155–64; Pramuk, *Sophia*, 200–202.

7. HGL, 115.

8. Thomas Merton, *Disputed Questions* (New York: Harcourt Brace, 1960), 65; hereafter DQ.

9. See Leonard Cohen, "Anthem," from the album *The Future* (Sony, 1992).

10. HGL, 564.

11. Martin Buber, *I and Thou*, trans. Walter Kaufman (New York: Touchstone, 1971).

12. Thomas Merton, *The Way of Chuang Tzu* (New York: New Directions, 1965), 130.

13. Walter Burghardt, "Contemplation: A Long Loving Look at the Real," in *An Ignatian Spirituality Reader* (Chicago: Loyola, 2008), 89–98.

14. For Merton's exposition of the "true self" and "false self," see Thomas Merton, *New Seeds of Contemplation* (New York: New Directions, 1961); hereafter NSC. Also James Finley, *Merton's Palace of Nowhere* (South Bend, IN: Ave Maria, 2003); and Anne Carr, *A Search for Wisdom and Spirit* (Notre Dame, IN: University of Notre Dame, 1988).

15. Thomas Merton, *Gandhi on Non-Violence: A Selection from the Writings of Mahatma Gandhi* (New York: New Directions, 1965), 5; hereafter GNV.

16. Martin Luther King Jr., *Strength to Love* (Philadelphia: Fortress Press, 1963), 72.

17. AJ, 308.

18. HGL, 566.

19. In her "Introduction" to *Thomas Merton: A Book of Hours* (Notre Dame, IN: Sorin, 2007), 15–42, Kathleen Deignan beautifully evokes the musicality and Psalm-like resonance of so much of Merton's corpus as a collective hymnody of praise, beckoning us, as she writes, through the "mythos gate" of revelatory speech (30).

20. The title of the final meditation in *New Seeds of Contemplation*, one of the most luminous and formally rendered of all the appearances of Wisdom-Sophia in Merton's corpus.

21. Andrew Louth, "Wisdom and the Russians: The Sophiology of Fr. Sergei Bulgakov," in *Where Shall Wisdom Be Found? Wisdom in the Bible, the Church, and the Contemporary World*, ed. Stephen C. Barton (Edinburgh: T& T Clark, 1999), 169–81, at 173. The literature on Wisdom-Sophia in the Jewish and Christian traditions is vast, rich, and not without controversy. For a superb overview, see Leo D. Lefebure, "The Wisdom of God: Sophia and Christian Theology," *Christian Century* 111, no. 29 (October 19, 1994): 951–57; in Christian feminist retrievals the definitive study is Elizabeth Johnson's magisterial *She Who Is: The Mystery of God in Feminist Theological Discourse* (New York: Crossroad, 1992).

22. The best introduction to Russian sophiology in English is Sergius Bulgakov's *Sophia: The Wisdom of God* (1937), the book that introduced

Merton to him. My own understanding is much indebted to Paul Valliere's *Modern Russian Theology: Bukharev, Soloviev, Bulgakov; Orthodox Theology in a New Key* (Grand Rapids, MI: T & T Clark, 2000), and numerous other sources cited in Pramuk, *Sophia*. Also deeply evocative and pivotal for Merton is Paul Evdokimov, *The Art of the Icon: A Theology of Beauty*, trans. Steven Bigham (Pasadena: Oakwood, 1989), esp. "The Icon of Divine Wisdom," 345–53.

23. Sergius Bulgakov, *Sophia: The Wisdom of God* (Hudson, NY: Lindisfarne, 1993), 21.

24. Bulgakov, cited in Valliere, *Modern Russian Theology*, 160. The question of God's freedom in relation to human freedom is central to Bulgakov's dogmatics of the "humanity of God." For Bulgakov the Son's incarnation respects "the *independence* of human nature in its freedom. Christ's humanity does not take the place of our natural humanity but co-lives, co-suffers, co-abides with it." The Spirit "'does not force human freedom but persuades it,' winning it over with patience and humility in an 'ongoing Pentecost' or 'final kenosis' which will continue until the end of the age" (332–33).

25. NSC, 296.

26. CGB, 11. The "erotic" dimension of the sophiological worldview follows from the testimony to *eros* in the Bible itself, or, better, Israel's *counter-testimony* to a different way of experiencing and speaking of YHWH than the prevailing or dominant testimony about God in the Hebrew Scriptures. As Walter Brueggemann observes, Proverbs 8 "imagines and articulates a way of God relating with the world that is not intrusive and occasional, but that is constant in its nurturing, sustaining propensity. It does indeed do 'God-talk' in a different tone, which witnesses to the mystery that can only be expressed as intuitive, playful, suggestive, doxological language, and which therefore necessarily opens the way for speculation about the precise relationship between the world and God." This sense of the "nurturing, sustaining propensity" of God—of God's "play" and "delight" in creation—"dares to expand and intensify the scope and depth of the claim made for Yahweh; *even before creation* . . . Yahweh assured that the world would be *fully permeated with an intentionality for life*." See Walter Brueggemann,

Theology of the Old Testament: Testimony, Dispute, Advocacy (Minneapolis: Fortress, 1997), 346, emphasis added; also Pramuk, *Sophia*, 250–56. On the prominent place of *eros* and the Song of Songs in the Christian mystical tradition, see Christopher Pramuk, "Sexuality, Spirituality, and the Song of Songs," *America* 193 (October 31, 2005): 8–12; Denys Turner, *Eros and Allegory: Medieval Exegesis of the Song of Songs* (Kalamazoo, MI: Cistercian Publications, 1995); Gillian T. Ahlgren, "Julian of Norwich's Theology of *Eros*," *Spiritus* 5, no. 1 (2005): 27–53; and George Kilcourse, "Spirituality as the Freedom to Channel Eros," *The Merton Annual* 13 (2000): 7–15.

27. See Merton's letter to Czeslaw Milosz, February 28, 1959, in *The Courage for Truth: The Letters of Thomas Merton to Writers*, ed. Christine M. Bochen (New York: Farrar, Straus and Giroux, 1993), 57–58; hereafter CT. See also Merton's striking meditations on Prometheus and Christ in *The Behavior of Titans* (New York: New Directions, 1961), 11–23. "Far from killing the man who seeks the divine fire, the Living God will Himself pass through death in order that man may have what is destined for him." Cf. "Promethean Theology," in *The New Man* (New York: Farrar, Straus and Giroux, 1961), 21–48.

28. NSC, 290; the following citations are from NSC, 296–97. Merton and the Russian theologians are careful to distinguish their intensely sacramental, sophianic view of creation from pantheism, monism, or materialist views of the natural world and human history. See Pramuk, *Sophia*, 99–100, 240–45.

III—pages 27–38

1. GNV, 6.
2. SFS, 85–86.
3. SFS, 87; cf. revised and expanded version, CGB, 21.
4. Lawrence S. Cunningham, *Thomas Merton and the Monastic Vision* (Grand Rapids, MI: Eerdmans, 1999), 55.
5. SFS, 176
6. CGB, 156, 158.

7. CT, 90.

8. ESF, 66–67.

9. Cited in Susan McCaslin, "Merton and 'Hagia Sophia,'" in *Merton and Hesychasm: Prayer of the Heart*, ed. Bernadete Dieker and Jonathan Montaldo (Louisville, KY: Fons Vitae, 2003), 234; hereafter MHPH.

10. Thomas Merton, *Witness to Freedom: The Letters of Thomas Merton in Times of Crisis*, ed. William H. Shannon (New York: Harcourt Brace, 1995), 4; hereafter WF. All citations from the letter in the following paragraphs are from WF, 4–5.

11. SJ, 361–62.

12. WF, 6.

13. Thomas Merton, *Turning Toward the World: The Pivotal Years*, vol. 4, ed. Victor A. Kramer (San Francisco: HarperSanFrancisco, 1997), 120; hereafter TTW.

14. TTW, 125.

15. TTW, 143–44.

16. TTW, 17–18.

17. Rowan Williams, "Bread in the Wilderness: The Monastic Ideal in Thomas Merton and Paul Evdokimov," in MHPH, 175–98, at 180.

18. TTW, 91.

19. Paul Evdokimov, *Woman and the Salvation of the World: A Christian Anthropology on the Charisms of Women*, trans. Anthony P. Gythiel (Crestwood, NY: St. Vladimir's Seminary Press, 1994), 230; see also SFS, 124, where Merton writes of Evdokimov, "How rare it is to find such theology!"

20. Prayer before the icon facilitates the re-centering of subjectivity from oneself to the divine, no longer related to as an object of self-fulfillment, but rather related to as Person and Presence. As iconographer William Hart McNichols writes, "You gaze on the icon, but it gazes on you too. We need to gaze on truly conversational, truly loving images, images that will return our love." Cited from www.fatherbill.org, where Fr. Bill's sophianic icons can also be viewed.

21. ESF, 61–62.

22. GNV, 1.

23. Christopher Nugent, "*Pax Heraclitus*: A Perspective on Merton's Healing Wholeness" (unpublished, 2005), 4; revised as "*Pax Heraclitus*: Heraclitus, Hagia Sophia, and a Hard Night's Peace," *The Merton Seasonal* 35, no. 2 (2010): 14–21.

24. From "God's Grandeur," in *Gerard Manley Hopkins: The Major Works* (Oxford: Oxford University Press, 1986), 128.

25. "Art when really understood is the province of every human being," writes American painter and teacher Robert Henri. "It is not an outside, extra thing. When the artist is alive in any person, whatever his kind of work may be, he becomes an inventive, searching, daring, self-expressing creature. He becomes interesting to other people. He disturbs, upsets, enlightens, and he opens ways for a better understanding. Where those who are not artists are trying to close the book, the artist opens it, shows there are still more pages possible." See *The Art Spirit* (New York: Basic Books, 2007; originally 1923), 11. Abraham Joshua Heschel speaks in a spirit very close to Merton and Henri when he advises young people, "And above all, remember that the meaning of life is to build life as if it were a work of art. You're not a machine. When you're young, start working on this great work of art called your own existence." Abraham Joshua Heschel, *Moral Grandeur and Spiritual Audacity* (New York: Farrar, Straus and Giroux, 1997), 412.

IV—pages 41–48

1. Mark S. Burrows, "Words That Reach into the Silence: Mystical Languages of Unsaying," in *Minding the Spirit: The Study of Christian Spirituality*, ed. Elizabeth A. Dreyer and Mark S. Burrows (Baltimore: Johns Hopkins, 2005), 213; citing Michael Sells.

2. My own citations are taken from *Emblems of a Season of Fury*, 61–69; the poem is also found in *A Thomas Merton Reader*, ed. Thomas P. McDonnell, rev. ed. (Garden City, NY: Doubleday, 1974), 506–11; Thomas Merton, *The Collected Poems of Thomas Merton* (New York: New Directions, 1977), 363–71; *Thomas Merton: Spiritual Master: The Essential*

Writings, ed. Lawrence Cunningham (New York: Paulist Press, 1992), 257–64; and Pramuk, *Sophia*, 301–5.

3. From "As Kingfishers Catch Fire," in *Gerard Manley Hopkins: The Major Works* (Oxford: Oxford University Press, 1986), 129.

4. ESF, 65; all citations from the poem in the following paragraphs from ESF 64–67.

5. McCaslin, MHPH, 248–49.

6. McCaslin, MHPH, 248.

7. McCaslin, MHPH, 248.

8. McCaslin, MHPH, 253.

9. In his lecture notes on Christian mysticism, Merton writes: "Mystical theology is not just [the] *via negationis*, apophatic theology, dialectical. It is beyond both forms of discursive theology, cataphatic and apophatic. It is the FULFILLMENT OF BOTH." See Thomas Merton, *An Introduction to Christian Mysticism: Initiation into the Monastic Tradition 3*, ed. Patrick F. O'Connell (Kalamazoo, MI: Cistercian, 2008), 142–43; hereafter ICM.

10. NSC, 29–36. Merton scholar Daniel P. Horan has also persuasively illuminated the Franciscan roots of Merton's spirituality and theological vision as expressed in this passage and many others. See "Thomas Merton the 'Dunce': Identity, Incarnation and the Not So Subtle Influence of John Duns Scotus," *Cistercian Studies Quarterly* 47 (May 2012): 149–75; and *The Franciscan Heart of Thomas Merton* (Notre Dame, IN: Ave Maria, 2014).

11. Patrick O'Connell, "Hagia Sophia," in *The Thomas Merton Encyclopedia*, ed. William H. Shannon, Christine M. Bochen, and Patrick F. O'Connell (Maryknoll, NY: Orbis, 2002), 191–93, at 192.

12. ESF, 68.

13. Margaret Bridge Betz, "Merton's Images of Elias, Wisdom, and the Inclusive God," in *The Merton Annual* 13, ed. George A. Kilcourse (Sheffield, UK: Sheffield Academic, 2001), 190–207, at 195. Also compelling is Betz's suggestion that the drawing, of uncertain date, may have been created as early as 1952, well before Merton began reading the Russian theologians.

14. HGL, 564.

15. Hiddenness was a favorite theme of Soloviev in his reflections on Sophia (McCaslin, MHPH, 241). Likewise, as noted above (II n. 26), Walter Brueggemann distinguishes Israel's "core testimony" to Yahweh's action in the world—"highly visible, evoking terror in the enemy and praise in the beneficiaries of that 'action'"—from Israel's "countertestimony," which emerges in three facets: hiddenness, ambiguity (or instability), and negativity (*Theology of the Old Testament*, 318); he associates Wisdom especially with the first, God's hiddenness in the world.

16. See Michael Mott, *The Seven Mountains of Thomas Merton* (Boston: Houghton Mifflin, 1984), 363.

V—pages 51–58

1. Thomas Merton, *Dancing in the Water of Life: Seeking Peace in the Hermitage*, ed. Robert E. Daggy (San Francisco: HarperSanFrancisco, 1997), 200; hereafter DWL.

2. DWL, 200.

3. DWL, 200–201.

4. DWL, 202.

5. ESF, 66.

6. Thomas Merton, *Learning to Love: Exploring Solitude and Freedom*, ed. Christine M. Bochen (San Francisco: HarperSanFrancisco, 1997), 328; hereafter LTL. "M." is the initial used to refer to the woman by Christine Bochen, the editor of the sixth volume of Merton's journals. Merton had stipulated through the Merton Legacy Trust that the private journals could be published twenty-five years after his death. Bochen is careful to remind readers that these passages give us access only to Merton's side of the story.

7. LTL, 130–31. For drawing attention to the connections between Wisdom-Sophia, Merton's drawings, and "M.," I am especially indebted to Jonathan Montaldo's important study, "A Gallery of Women's Faces and Dreams of Women from the Drawings and Journals of Thomas Merton," in *The Merton Annual* 14, ed. Victor A. Kramer (Sheffield, UK: Sheffield Academic Press, 2001), 172.

8. LTL, 329.

9. LTL, 329.

10. LTL, 328.

11. From "Love for God and Mutual Charity," MHPH, 447–72, at 454.

12. From Boris Pasternak's *Dr. Zhivago*, a seminal work for Merton, cited in DQ, 66–67.

13. Sergius Bulgakov, cited in SFS, 104.

14. From *Hagia Sophia*, ESF, 64.

VI—pages 61–69

1. Iconographer William Hart McNichols (Fr. Bill to many) shared with me that when Sophia first dawned in his consciousness some thirty years ago, she came "much more as a flashing red light than as a pleasant apparition." Conversation with the author, March 2010.

2. TTW, 91.

3. Alfred Delp to Luise Oestreicher, November 17, 1944; cited in *Ultimate Price: Testimonies of Christians Who Resisted the Third Reich*, selected by Annemarie S. Kidder (Maryknoll, NY: Orbis, 2012), 65–66.

4. ESF, 61.

5. DQ, 20–21.

6. Rowan Williams, *A Silent Action: Engagements with Thomas Merton* (Louisville: Fons Vitae, 2011), 19; citing Merton in SJ, 187.

7. Williams, *A Silent Action*, 19.

8. Williams, *A Silent Action*, 19.

9. Williams, *A Silent Action*, 19. For an appreciation of Williams' work on Merton, see Christopher Pramuk, "Poetic Priest to Poetic Priest," *The Living Church* 245, no. 2 (July 15, 2012): 21–24.

10. Of course, this is the most serious of questions for the religious believer. And yet with Merton somehow it is also a playful question, a joyful question, and not-so-serious. See Rowan Williams, "'Not Being Serious': Thomas Merton and Karl Barth," in *A Silent Action*, 71–82.

11. McCaslin, MHPH, 252.

12. McCaslin, MHPH, 253.

13. Biblical scholars have long recognized the Hebrew Wisdom foundations of New Testament Christology and almost certainly of Jesus' self-identity. For a sensitive introduction, see Marcus Borg, *Meeting Jesus again for the First Time: The Historical Jesus and the Heart of Contemporary Faith* (New York: HarperCollins, 1995), 69–118. James D. G. Dunn provides a balanced summary of the issues and texts at play in his *Christology in the Making: A New Testament Inquiry into the Origins of the Doctrine of the Incarnation* (Grand Rapids, MI: Eerdmans, 1996), 163–212.

14. ESF, 65–67.

15. See William Lynch, *Images of Hope: Imagination as Healer of the Hopeless* (Baltimore: Helicon, 1965).

16. HGL, 566.

VII—pages 71–85

1. Etty Hillesum, *An Interrupted Life and Letters from Westerbork* (New York: Henry Holt, 1996), 135–36.

2. Robert Ellsberg, *All Saints: Daily Reflections on Saints, Prophets, and Witnesses from Our Time* (New York: Crossroad, 1997), 522.

3. Hillesum, *An Interrupted Life*, 176.

4. Hillesum, *An Interrupted Life*, 171.

5. Hillesum, *An Interrupted Life*, 178. Compare to the preface of *Raids on the Unspeakable*, in which Merton describes the book's central message as "to be human in this most inhuman of ages, *to guard the image of man for it is the image of God*" (RU, 6).

6. Ellsberg, *All Saints*, 522.

7. Hillesum, *An Interrupted Life*, 360.

8. Melissa Raphael, *The Female Face of God in Auschwitz: A Jewish Feminist Theology of the Holocaust* (New York: Routledge, 2003).

9. Raphael, *Female Face of God*, 35. Raphael's thesis, rendered with considerable care and deference to the horrors of Auschwitz, hinges on the need to challenge patriarchal assumptions about how God's power

and presence are (and are not) manifest in the world: "There has been too much asking 'where was God in Auschwitz?' and not enough 'who was God in Auschwitz?'" (54).

10. Raphael, *Female Face of God*, 68.

11. Raphael, *Female Face of God*, 157.

12. Raphael, *Female Face of God*, 58.

13. Raphael, *Female Face of God*, 58.

14. Raphael, *Female Face of God*, 71.

15. Raphael, *Female Face of God*, 74; with a nod to Rudolph Otto's famous description (*The Idea of the Holy*) of religious experience as the *mysterium tremendum et fascinans*.

16. Raphael, *Female Face of God*, 139.

17. George Steiner, "To Speak of Walter Benjamin," in *Benjamin Studies: Perception and Experience in Modernity* (Amsterdam: Rodopi, 2002), 13–23, at 22.

18. Raphael, *Female Face of God*, 80.

19. Raphael, *Female Face of God*, 142.

20. Raphael, *Female Face of God*, 142.

21. Sergius Bulgakov, cited in Bernice Rosenthal, "The Nature and Function of Sophia in Sergei Bulgakov's Prerevolutionary Thought," in *Russian Religious Thought*, ed. Judith Kornblatt and Richard Gustafson (Madison: University of Wisconsin, 1996), 154–75, at 167. Bulgakov's constructive theology of the physical cosmos presages contemporary environmental and process theologies by some fifty years. "The fate of nature, suffering and awaiting its liberation, is henceforth connected with the fate of man. . . . The new heaven and new earth now enter as a necessary element into the composition of Christian eschatology." See *Sophia*, 240–50.

22. Hillesum, *An Interrupted Life*, 152.

23. Raphael, *Female Face of God*, 58; citing Victor Frankl, *Man's Search for Meaning*, 69. Raphael is careful to distinguish between the Jewish memory of Shekhinah as "the real presence of a suffering God" and a "quasi-Christian incarnation of God crucified in Auschwitz." In Jewish understanding, "the suffering is that of one who, being among us, suffers

with us, but does not suffer vicariously *for* us" (54–55). To be sure, great care must be taken not to simply conflate Jewish and Christian interpretations of a suffering God, particularly in the case of the Holocaust. Much depends from the Christian side on precisely *how* we understand Jesus' crucifixion to be redemptive.

24. For a powerful account of "womanist" interpretations of the Bible, see Diana Hayes, *Forged in the Fiery Furnace: African American Spirituality* (Maryknoll, NY: Orbis, 2012), 137–67. For a meditative, earthy, and often humorous reading of the "hidden women" of the New Testament, see Kathy Coffey, *The Hidden Women of the Gospel* (Maryknoll, NY: Orbis, 2003).

25. Maya Angelou, *The Complete Collected Poems of Maya Angelou* (New York: Random House, 1994), 163–64.

26. See Rosanne Murphy, *Martyr of the Amazon: The Life of Sister Dorothy Stang* (Maryknoll, NY: Orbis, 2007); Somaly Mam, *The Road of Lost Innocence: The True Story of a Cambodian Heroine* (New York: Spiegal and Grau, 2008); Nicolas Kristof and Sheryl Wu Dunn, *Half the Sky: Turning Oppression into Opportunity for Women Worldwide* (New York: Vintage, 2010); Maya Angelou, *The Complete Collected Poems of Maya Angelou* (New York: Random House, 1994), 163; Georges Bernanos, *The Diary of a Country Priest*, trans. Pamela Morris (New York: MacMillan, 1937); Sojourner Truth, "Ain't I A Woman" (http://www.fordham.edu/halsall/mod/sojtruth-woman.asp); Sue Monk Kidd, *The Secret Life of Bees* (New York: Penguin, 2003).

27. Rita Gross, cited in Raphael, *Female Face of God*, 150. In a similar spirit, Kristof and Wu Dunn open their study of global women's oppression (n. 26) with a Chinese proverb: *Women hold up half the sky.*

28. See *Thomas Merton: Selected Essays*, ed. Patrick F. O'Connell (Maryknoll, NY: Orbis, 2013), 39–51.

29. Several years ago pastors at Catholic churches in Arizona, Michigan, and Virginia forbade altar girls during all forms of the Mass—not just the reinstated Tridentine form—under the logic that "replacing girls with boys as servers leads to more vocations to the priesthood." Facing objections from parishioners, a Phoenix pastor says he did not consult the

parish council "because they are not theologically trained." Editors, "Save the Altar Girls," *America* (October 10, 2011); Tom Gallagher, "No Girl Servers at Latin Masses," *National Catholic Reporter Online* (June 9, 2011); Alice Popovici, "Catholics Protest Altar Server Policy," *National Catholic Reporter Online* (December 3, 2011). Though it is still early in his papacy Pope Francis has been an outspoken critic of clericalism and has suggested that "we don't yet have a truly deep theology of women in the church."

30. Wisdom 8:16, from Merton's fiftieth birthday journal, January 31, 1965 (DWL, 200–201).

31. CGB, 212. For Islamic perspectives on divine-human relationality and the divine feminine, see Seyyed Hossein Nasr, "The Male and Female in the Islamic Perspective," *Studies in Comparative Religion* 14, nos. 1–2 (Winter–Spring, 1980); and Laurence Galian, "The Centrality of the Divine Feminine in Sufism," *Proceedings of the 2nd Annual Hawaii International Conference on Arts and Humanities* (2004), http://www.hichumanities.org/. On the sacramental imagination and hope rising from the remembrance of God as Wisdom-Sophia, see Christopher Pramuk, "Presences," in *Hope Sings, So Beautiful: Graced Encounters across the Color Line* (Collegeville, MN: Liturgical Press, 2013), 105–21.

VIII—pages 87–95

1. SJ, 341.

2. Howard Thurman, *With Head and Heart: The Autobiography of Howard Thurman* (New York: Harcourt Brace, 1979), 226.

3. Howard Thurman, *Howard Thurman: Essential Writings*, selected with an introduction by Luther E. Smith (Maryknoll, NY: Orbis, 2006), 39; hereafter HTEW.

4. HTEW, 39.

5. HTEW, 38.

6. Psychologist Abraham Maslow described the "peak experience" as a state of blissfulness more or less characteristic of natural processes of self-actualization and innately available to everyone. Researcher Edith

Cobb developed her groundbreaking theory of the "ecology of imagination in childhood" after discovering striking similarities in the biographies of some three hundred artistic or "creative geniuses," each of whom had experienced their natural surroundings in an intense, life-determining way as a child.

7. HTEW, 40; Abraham Joshua Heschel, *Man Is Not Alone: A Philosophy of Religion* (New York: Farrar, Straus and Young, 1951), 75.

8. HTEW, 41.

9. HTEW, 66.

10. HTEW, 68–69.

11. HTEW, 61.

12. HTEW, 69.

13. HTEW, 41.

14. Thomas Merton, *Seasons of Celebration* (New York: Farrar, Straus and Giroux, 1965), 118.

15. While speech itself in the Jewish tradition is an efficacious form of action, Heschel also insisted that human beings as God's image in the world stand under the divine imperative to act, to set our labors against evil, to create of our lives in partnership with God works of divine-human art. We are called not just to see and speak the truth but *to act* with compassion and justice, in Christian terms, to follow the way of the cross. On living in the boundary between contemplative speech (poetry) and political activism, see Susan McCaslin, "Pivoting toward Peace: The Engaged Poetics of Thomas Merton and Denise Levertov," in *The Merton Annual*, vol. 22 (Louisville: Fons Vitae, 2009), 189–203. Of her own political activism Levertov writes: "When words penetrate deep into us they change the chemistry of the soul, of the imagination. We have no right to do that to people if we don't share the consequences."

16. Cited in Edward K. Kaplan, *Holiness in Words: Abraham Joshua Heschel's Poetics of Piety* (Albany: State University of New York, 1996), 16.

17. Abraham Joshua Heschel, *Man Is Not Alone: A Philosophy of Religion* (New York: Farrar, Straus and Young, 1951), 35.

IX—pages 97–109

1. Cited in GNV, 25.

2. See RU, 71.

3. Maya Angelou, *Interview with the Academy of Achievement* (1990). Accessed at http://www.achievement.org/autodoc/page/ang0int-2.

4. Steven Weitzman, *Solomon: The Lure of Wisdom* (New Haven, CT: Yale University Press, 2011), 2–3.

5. RU, 75.

6. Ian Johnston, "Malala Yousafzai: Being Shot by the Taliban Made Me Stronger," accessed August 1, 2014, at http://www.nbcnews.com/news/other/malala-yousafzai-being-shot-taliban-made-me-stronger-f6C10612024.

7. When Kristof and Wu Dunn (VII n. 26 above) ask "Is Islam Misogynistic?" (*Half the Sky*, 149–66), they pose one of the more important theological questions of our time, with far-reaching social and political implications. Of course, whether Christianity or Catholicism is misogynistic in essence or practice also must continue to be asked.

8. Kevin Clarke, "Outrage Again," *America* 210, no. 20 (June 23–30, 2014).

9. John Jay College Research Team, "The Causes and Context of Sexual Abuse of Minors by Catholic Priests in the United States, 1950–2010" (May 2011), http://old.usccb.org/mr/causes-and-context.shtml.

10. The image I borrow from "Mild He Lays His Glory By" (anonymous), in *No One's Easy Daughter: Life Journeys Behind and Beyond the Veil* (forthcoming). The notion of "social sin" or "institutional sin" in Catholic doctrine (*Catechism of the Catholic Church*, nos. 1849–69) is crucial to any discussion of freedom and the mystery of personal and social evil, whether manifest in society or church. "There are no islands [where we do not already] bear the stamp of the guilt of others, directly or indirectly, from close or from afar" (Karl Rahner, *Foundations of Christian Faith* [New York: Crossroads, 1978], 109). In the Christian mystical tradition, the cultivation of "purity of heart" and "poverty of spirit" through the life of prayer and "docility to the Holy Spirit" in all things is our enduring defense against

the lure of the evil spirit. See Johann Baptist Metz, *Poverty of Spirit* (New York: Paulist Press, 1998).

11. Bill McKibben, *The End of Nature* (New York: Random House, 1989), esp. 40–60. "We never thought that we had wrecked nature. Deep down, we never really thought we could: it was too big and too old; its forces—the wind, the rain, the sun—were too strong, too elemental. . . . . But now the basis of that faith is lost." The broad impact of McKibben's prophetic work has been compared to that in Merton's generation of Rachel Carson's *Silent Spring*. Like Carson—and like Pope Francis in his linking of environmental devastation with unrestrained global capitalism—McKibben has been vilified by established economic interests even while his ecological conclusions have been vindicated by climate science. For the latest research, see Intergovernmental Panel on Climate Change (IPCC), *Climate Change 2014*, accessible at http://www.ipcc.ch/index.htm.

12. Walter Brueggemann, *The Prophetic Imagination*, 2nd ed. (Minneapolis: Augsburg Fortress Press, 2001), 63–64.

13. Edward Kaplan, "Introduction," in Abraham Joshua Heschel, *The Ineffable Name of God: Man* (New York: Continuum, 2005), 7–18, at 15. On the negative effects of globalization, see Pope Francis, *Evangelii Gaudium*, especially nos. 52–75, 186–237.

14. From Thomas Merton, "Poetry and Contemplation: A Reappraisal," in *The Literary Essays of Thomas Merton*, ed. Patrick Hart (New York: New Directions, 1981), 340. Cf. Walter Brueggemann, *Finally Comes the Poet: Daring Speech for Proclamation* (Minneapolis: Fortress, 1989).

15. SFS, 85–86.

16. SFS, 85–86.

17. As in Victor Hammer's icon, where she crowns the boy Jesus (see Prov 4:8-9).

18. SFS, 182. From Merton's letter to "Proverb," following her unexpected "epiphany" in the passersby at a busy street corner in Louisville.

19. "You've got to have images. The imagination has got to have some part of a balanced diet. . . . Scripture has great images. . . . One of the great graces of my life, as far as this question of being imaginative goes, is

the fact of having more or less grown up among European cathedrals and monasteries and things like that. I mean to have all that around you when you are a kid is marvelous. And to grow up with that sort of stuff and with that kind of imagery, you see" (MHPH, 461). As Merton here intimates, at stake in the renewal of speech about God is our need for vibrant conceptual models *and* images in the spiritual life of the community. But the models (theology, Christology, pneumatology, Mariology) and images (Father, Mother, Child, Friend) serve us well insofar as they make real or help us to realize (i.e. sacramentalize) fundamental *ways of being* in the world, our co-participation in God's own Being. In *Sophia*, I develop this integral link between theology and spirituality under the language of "Presence." God in Jesus is revealed as boundless Mercy, Compassion, Loving Presence. A Wisdom-saturated Christology (theology, ecclesiology) of Presence helps us live and breathe as persons and as church from the essential core and good news of the faith (*Sophia*, 211, 257–65). My book *Hope Sings, So Beautiful* might also be described as a sustained meditation on the possibilities of Presence, a kind of applied spirituality of Presense as related to crossing boundaries of race and gender in society and church.

20. Here again I am indebted to Susan McCaslin's rich exegesis of the poem, "Merton and 'Hagia Sophia,'" in MHPH, 235–54.

21. Kwok Pui-lan, "Mending of Creation: Women, Nature, and Eschatological Hope," in *Liberating Eschatology: Essays in Honor of Letty M. Russell*, ed. Margaret Farley and Serene Jones (Louisville: Westminster John Knox, 1999), 144–55, at 150. Pui-lan's discussion of the sex trade throws the vision of Sophia into a darkly urgent and apocalyptic light. In far too many places of the world, gays and lesbians too, it must be said, live under the shadow of constant threat and "have their histories inscribed on their bodies." For my own attempt to think and pray through the questions raised by gender and sexual difference, see "Imagination and Difference: Beyond Essentialism in Church Teaching and Practice," *New Theology Review* 26, no. 1 (2013): 42–52; online at http://newtheologyreview.com /index.php/ntr/article/view/51/1226.

22. Roger Haight, *Jesus Symbol of God* (Maryknoll, NY: Orbis, 1999), 293. "From a theological perspective, Jesus could have been a woman, and to make specific theological points from the facticity of his manhood without further warrant would seem to be fundamentally wrong."

23. Sandra Schneiders, *Women and the Word: The Gender of God in the New Testament and the Spirituality of Women* (New York: Paulist Press, 1986), 19. To be sure, all the images and questions at play here must be "framed" (without being bound!) in terms of christological and trinitarian doctrine, liturgy, interfaith dialogue, and all other manner of church practices, tasks that occupied Bulgakov for much of his extraordinary career and that I explore schematically in *Sophia*, especially chapter 6. In other words, the image will give rise to new (and the retrieval of ancient) forms of thought but also to new (and the retrieval of ancient) liturgical forms, rites, and ways of being in the community.

24. ESF, 63–64.

25. NSC, 297.

26. Susan McCaslin, "Thomas Merton, Citizen of the World," in *We Are Already One: Thomas Merton's Message of Hope* (Louisville: Fons Vitae, 2015), 33.